Labor Arbitration
in America

LABOR ARBITRATION IN AMERICA

The Profession and Practice

Edited by Mario F. Bognanno and Charles J. Coleman

A Project of the Research Committee
of the National Academy of Arbitrators,
Funded Jointly by the NAA and the NAA Research
and Education Foundation

New York
Westport, Connecticut
London

Library of Congress Cataloging-in-Publication Data

Labor arbitration in America : the profession and practice / edited by
Mario F. Bognanno and Charles J. Coleman.
    p. cm.
    "A project of the Research Committee of the National Academy of
Arbitrators."
    Includes index.
    ISBN 0-275-94375-5 (alk. paper)
    1. Arbitration, Industrial—United States. I. Bognanno, Mario
Frank. II. Coleman, Charles J. III. National Academy of
Arbitrators. Committee on Research.
    HD5504.A3L28 1992
    331.89'143'0973—dc20   92-399

British Library Cataloguing in Publication Data is available.

Library of Congress Catalog Card Number: 92-399
ISBN: 0-275-94375-5

First published in 1992

Praeger Publishers, One Madison Avenue, New York, NY 10010
An imprint of Greenwood Publishing Group, Inc.

Printed in the United States of America

The paper used in this book complies with the
Permanent Paper Standard issued by the National
Information Standards Organization (Z39.48-1984).

10 9 8 7 6 5 4 3 2 1

Contents

Preface

Arbitration has been around, in one form or another, since biblical times but, over the last fifty years, it has become a fundamental part of the American labor relations system. Despite the field's age and its contemporary importance, surprisingly little is known about the people who call themselves arbitrators and about characteristics of their arbitration practices.

The Research Committee of the National Academy of Arbitrators (NAA) decided that it was time to fill this gap in knowledge. The Board of Governors of the Academy and the NAA Research and Education Foundation agreed to fund the most comprehensive study on the practice and profession of arbitration that has ever been undertaken in the United States. Members of the NAA Research Committee spent months designing an instrument to provide definitive answers to a number of basic questions about arbitration and the people who practice it, gathering data from a sample that was representative of the arbitration population, and codifying and analyzing these data.

The initial data collection and analysis phases of this research were handled by the Survey Research Center, Iowa State University, and the Industrial Relations Center, University of Minnesota. More recently, several other universities with which some of the book's authors are affiliated supported the computer analysis dictated by their individual chapter needs.

This book has two very ambitious objectives. The first was to produce an empirical study about arbitrators and arbitration that was more complete, richly textured, and analytical than has ever been completed up to this time. This was not an attempt to add one more book to the already voluminous literature on the law of arbitration, standards, evidence, or how to present a case. The goal was to tell an untold story about labor arbitration and the people who practice it.

In a limited sense, this story is about arbitration as it was in 1986 and 1987—the years about which the NAA database was assembled. However, in a general sense, this report is current because many of the characteristics captured by the database are enduring or long-term in nature. For instance, a number of years may elapse before the nature of the people practicing arbitration will undergo significant demographic changes or their geographic distribution will shift. Observed differences will change slowly, if at all, in areas such as the proportion of full-time to part-time arbitrators; the comparative caseloads of Academy and non-Academy members; or the proportion of arbitrators who earn in excess of, say, $50,000 or more per year (in constant dollars).

Some characteristics do change more rapidly, and in those areas the information in the study provides a basis for drawing future comparisons. For example, the share of women or minority group members in arbitration may change from one year to another. Thus, baseline 1986–87 information about such dynamic features of the profession may be "dated." Nevertheless, in some of these areas, the reported data are the best information currently available on the topic; and, of equal importance, they provide a critical baseline against which the findings of later studies can be compared.

The second objective was to create a "user friendly" book—one that could be easily understood by academics and non-academics, arbitrators and interested observers of the process. Without compromising academic rigor this book stays away from the sophisticated statistical models and tests, concentrating instead on telling the story honestly but plainly.

This book casts new light on a series of questions that have never before been answered fully about the numbers of arbitrators practicing in the United States; their backgrounds, experiences, and aspirations; the differences between NAA and non-NAA arbitrators; how the arbitration career develops; the issues with which arbitrators deal; cases and from whence they come; arbitration earnings—"feast or famine"; whether a future shortage of arbitrators can be anticipated; and where the profession is going as the twenty-first century approaches.

A serious attempt was made to produce a reasonably integrated study. Reflecting the multifaceted nature of the arbitration profession, the authors come from a variety of backgrounds. They are all academically based practicing arbitrators and members of the NAA. But their backgrounds span engineering, theoretical and institutional economics, industrial relations, human resource management, and law. Left completely alone, they easily could have produced a set of essays bound together only by the front and back covers of this book. However, the editors attempted to select the various topics covered, integrate inter-topic analyses and reduce overlap, while giving each author the right to complete a freestanding chapter.

Many people played uniquely important roles in bringing about this book. The initial push for this project came from Mark Kahn, then president of the NAA. The full breadth of subjects to be examined was fleshed out during John Dunsford's and William Fallon's terms as president. These leaders and their successors provided the encouragement required of an enterprise like this. Indeed, the Academy's Board joined Alex Elson, then president of the NAA Research and Education Foundation, to provide the funds needed to launch it. This was the first research endeavor to be funded by the Foundation. Subsequently, large chunks of "in kind" support were provided by the Industrial Relations Center, University of Minnesota, and Iowa State University.

Marcia Greenbaum generously shared her expertise and critique with Mario Bognanno and Clifford Smith, the two responsible for putting together the survey questionnaire. For designing the survey instrument and methodology, Tony Genalo and Roy Hickman from Iowa State's Survey Research Center warrant special acknowledgment. Diana Beck, Young Myon Lee, and Shafi Khaled, all graduate students in Industrial Relations at the University of Minnesota, helped to create the data files underlying the analyses reported in this volume's chapters. Mary Alice Schumacher of the University of Minnesota provided editing and word processing assistance.

While this project began and ended during Bognanno's terms as Chair of the NAA Committee on Research, the bridging terms were chaired by Clifford Smith. It was Smith who energized the project when interest faded and guided much of the co-editors' work. To him go very special thanks. Lastly, Gladys W. Gruenberg, Professor Emerita of Economics and Industrial Relations, St. Louis University, performed a great service by reading the manuscript cover-to-cover, making significant improvements along the way. We are forever in her debt.

Mario F. Bognanno
Charles J. Coleman

Labor Arbitration
in America

1

Introduction to the NAA Survey

Clifford E. Smith

Introduction and Background of the Study

The resolution of disputes through the use of a neutral third party is an age-old practice. But even though history records many occasions where individuals asked some third party to help them resolve a dispute, it is only since the 1940s that neutrals, other than the courts, have come to play an important role in dispute resolution in the United States. In the field of labor relations, third parties have taken on an extremely significant role as arbitrators. Partially as a result of this success, arbitration has also increased in other fields including construction, insurance and product liability claims, and even family disputes.

While the practice of arbitrating labor disputes is common today and an extensive body of arbitration law has developed since the 1940s, little is known about the people who act as arbitrators and the practice of arbitration. As the next chapter shows, almost all of the existing studies of arbitrators were built on narrow databases. They were generally limited to arbitrators in a given geographic area, to members of the National Academy of Arbitrators (NAA), or to those who had decisions published by the Bureau of National Affairs (BNA). Prior to this study, there were no conclusive answers to such questions as: What types of backgrounds do arbitrators possess? What kinds of practices do they have? How many cases do they decide and how much money do they earn? Are there geographical differences in the practice of arbitration? Do the practices of members of the NAA differ from the practices of nonmembers? How are women and minorities doing in the field? Prior to this study, no one even had a definitive estimate of the number of people in the United States who claimed to be professional arbitrators.

This dearth of information about arbitrators and the arbitration practice was recognized by the Research Committee of the National Academy of Arbitrators when it published, in 1986, an annotated bibliography on arbitration.[1] The editors noted that none of the 590 studies cited were based on information about the *population* of arbitrators in the United States. Furthermore, Bognanno and Smith reported in 1989 that: "The demographic and behavioral research is limited to small sets of arbitrators, such as NAA members, labor panels of the Federal Mediation and Conciliation Service (FMCS) and the American Arbitration Association (AAA), or practitioners in a specific geographic area."[2]

The NAA Research Committee (hereafter, the Committee) identified two research needs: (1) to develop a database on the demographics and the professional practices of all arbitrators; and (2) to establish baseline statistics against which future data could be compared to measure the nature and extent of change in labor arbitration. The Committee proposed to gather a wide range of data that should, at a minimum, provide accurate estimates of the number of labor arbitrators in the United States and Canada and if they were practicing full-time or part-time. The study would draw the demographic profile of arbitrators, provide information on their education and employment background, and indicate career paths. The study would also estimate the utilization (caseloads) of arbitrators and the economics of being an arbitrator. In late 1987 the Board of Governors of the NAA Arbitrators and the NAA Research and Education Foundation authorized the Committee to conduct a "baseline census" on the "Characteristics and Practices of Professional Labor Arbitrators in the United States and Canada" and provided funding. This research effort is the foundation upon which this book rests.

This chapter summarizes the methodology employed in the study, describes the questionnaire that was used, addresses questions about representativeness, and closes with a few words on arbitration as a profession. Each of the additional chapters presents an analytical essay based on part of the information gathered in this survey. While each chapter may be read individually and is complete in its own right, together they provide the first definitive answers to the questions raised prior to this study.

Because of the important message being conveyed, this book has been written for a general audience—for non-academics as well as academics, for non-arbitrators as well as arbitrators. The rigor of the analysis has not been compromised, but scientific jargon and sophisticated models and statistical tests have been avoided. The authors have taken this approach, not because they are unfamiliar with the techniques, but because, as Hawking has said, each formula cuts the audience by half.[3]

Background on Labor Arbitration

Arbitration is the process of submitting a controversy between two parties or organizations to a neutral third party for final and binding resolution. Two basic forms of arbitration have emerged in labor-management relations. The first, *interest arbitration*, is concerned with disputes *over* the future terms and conditions of a labor contract. In the United States, many state and federal laws require this form of arbitration when the parties engaged in negotiation for a public sector collective bargaining reach an impasse.

But it is the second form of arbitration, *rights arbitration*, that has spread so rapidly and widely in both public and private sector labor relations over the past five decades. Rights arbitration differs from interest arbitration in two respects. First, it is applied to disputes over the interpretation and application of an existing collective bargaining agreement, rather than the negotiation of a new one; and, second, it is most often voluntary rather than mandatory, because the parties have freely contracted to accept the decision of a neutral.

Despite its newfound prominence, however, arbitration is not a new development in labor-management relations.[4] As long ago as 1824, for example, the British Parliament established a method of settling "wage disputes either by tribunals set up voluntarily by the parties or through the courts, if they failed to act."[5] The first recorded instance of voluntary arbitration in the United States took place in 1865 in a dispute involving the iron puddlers of Pittsburgh.

Arbitration was used initially to settle strikes or disputes over the terms and working conditions of a contract. But after its use by the War Labor Boards during the first and second World Wars, it became the preferred method for resolving disputes that arose over an existing labor contract. The use of this form of arbitration was encouraged by President Truman's National Labor-Management Conference of 1945 when it recommended that disputes involving the interpretation or application of an agreement be resolved "by an impartial chairman, umpire, arbitrator, or board."[6]

Since the 1940s, the use of voluntary arbitration has become the accepted way of settling disputes between employers and employee organizations. Its use has been supported through the decisions of the National Labor Relations Boards, public agencies entrusted with the enforcement of state labor laws and local ordinances, and by all levels of the judiciary. Reflecting on private sector developments, Loewenberg reported that by the 1950s, more than 90 percent of labor agreements provided for arbitration of unresolved employee grievances.[7] That percentage is undoubtedly higher today. Binding arbitration of grievances came later to the public sector, but it has become an established part of labor relations in the U.S. Postal Service, is required in all contracts negotiated under the federal government's Civil Service Reform Act of 1978, and has been authorized or required in almost all of the public employee collective bargaining laws that have been passed over the last three decades.[8]

The Significance of the Study

This is an important study for several reasons. Consider for a moment the nature and extent to which arbitration and arbitrators are used today in the United States. Chapter 5 will show that in the base year of the NAA study (1986), almost 65,000 grievances of unionized and non-unionized employees came to arbitration, as did some 3,000 interest and mediation-arbitration (med-arb) cases, and almost 1,500 Alternative Dispute Resolution (ADR) cases. In addition, arbitrators mediated almost 4,000 United States labor disputes and served as fact-finders on 2,000 occasions (Table 5.4). The size of these numbers testifies to the obvious importance of the arbitration process to the economy, the society, and the interests of effective administration and social justice. However, there is no reasonably comprehensive, contemporary analysis of the characteristics of this profession and the people who practice it. There is a yawning gap in the literature that begs to be filled.

This study fills this gap quite well. First, this is an empirical study drawing on a large database. The authors analyze more information on arbitrators and the arbitration process than has been gathered for any prior study. The size of the database goes a long way toward explaining the delay between the time the data were gathered and the time this book went to press. Fortunately, however, this is not an exercise in ancient history. The kinds of behavioral, demographic, and economic characteristics studied do not change very rapidly and the analytical questions asked in this book have not been answered in the intervening years.

Second, the study has been designed to produce generalizable results. The study sample is not only large in its own right, but it was designed to be representative of the arbitration population. As shown in more detail later in this chapter, the sample was constructed in such a way that all of the major segments of the arbitration population were represented in proportion to their numbers in that population. The data include large numbers of NAA members and nonmembers, young and old, highly experienced and less experienced arbitrators, and so forth. There are a very large number of white men in the study, as can be expected, but there are also a fair number of women and a sprinkling of minority arbitrators. There is a sound basis for concluding that the insights shared here do, in fact, apply to the contemporary arbitration population.

Finally, this study is distinguished by the breadth and the depth of coverage and the importance of the questions asked. This book examines not only the backgrounds of arbitrators, but their aspirations, careers, caseloads, and earnings. It examines where their cases come from, the issues they confront, and the shape of the future. Furthermore, the contributing authors do more than describe. They raise analytical questions about the hallmark characteristics of arbitrators and the arbitration process, and they explore topics of great contemporary concern, including the inroads made by women and minorities into this traditionally white male profession, the role and the impact of the National Academy of Arbitrators, and whether a shortage of arbitrators can be expected in the coming years.

Methodology

The Questionnaire

The members of the Committee created 47 questions to obtain the data necessary to respond to the issues that had been raised. The first questions dealt with demographic characteristics and training and education. The respondents were then asked to indicate their affiliation with professional organizations, and the location of their office(s). This was followed by questions concerning the events that triggered their entry into the profession, their occupation at that time, and any employment experience either with a labor organization or in industrial relations/human resources (IR/ HR).

Question 19 asked if the arbitrator worked on interest and/or grievance arbitration cases in 1986 and if this was on a "full-time" or "part-time" basis. Arbitrators who did not work in 1986 were asked: "Why not?" In later analysis, those who were not in active practice would be separated from active arbitrators.

The remaining questions dealt with the arbitrator's practice in 1986. Information was requested about caseloads, number of cases received from listing services, from direct selections, umpireships, and panels. Respondents were asked about the number of cases they decided five years prior and what they would like their caseload to be in 1987 and 1990. Information was requested on the arbitrator's fee schedule, as well as the total days billed in 1986. Finally, questions were asked on the distribution of cases by issues, by types of industry, and by geographic locations. In closing, respondents indicated their involvement with alternative dispute resolution (ADR) in 1986 and what they expected of ADR in the future. A copy of the questionnaire is provided in the first Appendix to the book.

The Mailing

Although there are many different arbitration rosters, there is no one listing of arbitrators in the United States which can be used for research purposes. Thus, one of the first challenges of the Committee was to develop a comprehensive list of people who were available to serve as arbitrators in labor-management disputes at the time the data were collected.

The common technique for selecting an arbitrator is to contact a federal, state, or private agency that maintains a list of persons whom the agency has determined to be arbitrators and who are available to serve. The two major listing agencies are the Federal Mediation and Conciliation Service, a federal agency, and the American Arbitration Association, a private, nonprofit organization. Most states also have agencies that deal with labor-management disputes, and each may maintain its own list of arbitrators.

The list employed in this study was prepared by writing first to all of the agencies thought to maintain a list of arbitrators for their clients. Sixty-one agencies were contacted, including the American Arbitration Association, the Federal Mediation and Conciliation Service, State Departments of Labor, Public Employee Relations Boards, Labor Relations Authorities, and Departments of Human Resources. All but six responded, and those who maintained a list of arbitrators provided the Committee with that information. The names of the agencies contacted are provided in the second Appendix to this book. In addition, the membership of the National Academy of Arbitrators was included, as were all names listed in the *Directory of U.S. Labor Arbitrators*.[9]

The Sampling Plan

Although the original list contained some 7,500 names, there were many duplications because most arbitrators list with more than one agency. After eliminating the duplicates and the Canadian arbitrators, a list of 4,127 United States arbitrators emerged.[10] This list was divided into two groups: one consisted of the 614 arbitrators who were then members of the NAA, and the other group consisted of the 3,513 non-NAA arbitrators.

Because this was an NAA study, the Committee wished to provide all Academy members with the opportunity to participate. Thus, the Committee sent questionnaires to all NAA members. Cost considerations prohibited a full population study of the non-NAA arbitrators, and consequently a 20 percent random sample was drawn, consisting of 702

Table 1.1
Estimated 1987 Total Population of Arbitrators in the United States

	NAA	Non-NAA	Total
(1) Population of Arbitrators in U.S. -- First Estimate	614	3,513	4,127
(2) Number in Sample	614	702	1,316
(3) Total Returns	376	389	765
(4) Reduced by Faulty Address/not usable	5	70	75
(5) Total Good Returns	371	319	690
(6) Noneligible Returns	13	57	70
(7) Percent Not Eligible of Total Returns	13/371 = 3.504%	57/319 17.868%	
(8) Estimated Number of Not Eligibles in Total Population Row 1 x Row 7 =	22	628	
(9) Therefore, Adjusted Population	592	2,885	3,477
(10) The Multiplier then is	592/358 = 1.6536	2,885/262 11.0114	

arbitrators stratified by geographic location (zip code).[11] On March 23, 1987, questionnaires were mailed to 614 NAA members and 702 non-NAA arbitrators, along with a letter explaining the purpose of the research. A follow-up postcard encouraging replies was mailed to non-respondents in April 1987.

Estimating the Population

Returns from these mailings provide the basis for the population estimate. Precisely 765 responses were received (row three of Table 1.1), 376 from NAA members and 389 from non-NAA arbitrators. Seventy-two of these were returned because of faulty or inaccurate address, and three were returned because the individual did not wish to respond (row four). These responses were retained in the population count on the assumption that they were bona fide arbitrators, but row five removes them from further study and indicates that the number of "good" returns totaled 690. Of these, 371 were NAA arbitrators and 319, non-NAA. Considering only these "good" returns, the response rate was 60.4 percent for NAA members and 45.4 percent for non-NAA arbitrators.

The first question asked was: "Have you ever been a neutral arbitrator?'' Those responding "no" were asked to return the questionnaire (row 6) without answering the remaining questions. Seventy questionnaires were returned. Thirteen of these were from NAA members, and the returned form indicated that they were either incapacitated or deceased. Some of the remaining 57 from the non-NAA list were also incapacitated or deceased, but many indicated that they were mediators or fact-finders, despite their presence on an arbitration list. Because these people were not currently arbitrators, they were deleted from the study and from the estimate of the total population.

On the assumption that the original population contained an equivalent number of persons who were not arbitrators or who were incapacitated or deceased, an estimate of the number of ineligibles from the original population was computed (row 8). This calculation determined that an adjusted estimate of the arbitrator population (row 9) was 592 NAA members and 2,885 non-NAA arbitrators.

The study group consists of 358 NAA members and 262 non-NAA arbitrators.[12] The next step was to weight the sample. As has been shown, the survey included all members of the National Academy, but only a twenty percent sample of all other arbitrators, and the response rate of the NAA arbitrators was much higher. Unless the responses were weighted to reflect these factors, the results would overemphasize the information provided by NAA arbitrators. Weights were assigned to each respondent based on the estimated population from which they were drawn—NAA and non-NAA populations (row 10). Each of the 358 NAA respondents represented 1.6536 members in the Academy, and each of the 262 non-NAA respondents represented 11.0114 arbitrators in the large set of all other arbitrators. These two numbers later will be used as expansion weights whenever NAA and non-NAA subsamples are combined to provide estimates pertaining to all arbitrators. Thus, each response from an Academy member is treated as 1.6536 responses, and each from a non-NAA arbitrator carries the weight of 11.0114 responses.

There has been a great deal of speculation on the number of arbitrators in the United States, but prior to this study there had been no definitive estimate. This study puts this matter to rest: in 1986 there were approximately 3,500 arbitrators in the United States and about 600 of these (17%) belonged to the NAA.

How Representative Is This Study?

No one is ever fully certain that a sample represents the population. But there are at least four reasons to support the contention that the sample developed in the NAA study did, in fact, fairly represent the United States arbitration population in 1986. These reasons are based upon methodology and size, comparison with other studies, and a priori knowledge of the arbitrator population.

Methodology and Size

As has been shown, the sample consisted of all of the members of the NAA plus a carefully selected, geographically stratified, random sample drawn from all of the arbitrators listed by the most active referral services in the United States. In addition, with roughly 360 NAA members and 260 nonmembers, the sample was both relatively large and reasonably balanced. Coupled with the carefully constructed sampling plan, a sample of this size and composition should produce results that are representative of the population.

Comparison with Other Studies

Certain characteristics of a population do not change rapidly or dramatically. If a group is largely male or older, it can be expected to remain that way unless a number of significant external factors change. If this study is representative, some of its results will reflect those enduring population characteristics reported in reputable older studies. Table 1.2 contrasts a number of results from this study with those from four earlier ones that are typical of the literature in this field.

The variables in the table are age, education, professional affiliation, and employment status. The 1971 McKelvey and Rogers study was based on a sample of NAA members; the 1977 work of Petersen and Rezler and the 1980 monograph of Briggs and Anderson were based upon geographically drawn samples (the Midwest and California, respectively); and the 1973 King analysis was drawn from capsule biographies published in *Labor Arbitration Reports*. Chapter 2 provides more information on these studies.

Despite the diversity of each study's population base, there is a high degree of consistency between comparable means in this study and those of the earlier works. For example, the mean age in the NAA sample is 58.4, which is almost the same as that reported by Briggs and Anderson, Petersen and Rezler, and King. The mean age of Academy members in this sample is close to 62, considerably higher than that reported by McKelvey and Rogers in 1969 (a mean age of 57). But the age of Academy members probably increased during the intervening years, as is indicated in the more extensive summary of NAA studies found in the next chapter.

Approximately 55 percent of arbitrators in this study have law degrees. This is very close to the findings by Petersen and Rezler (59%). A lower figure (45%) was reported by Briggs and Anderson, but they also reported that their estimate was incorrect because prior information showed that

Table 1.2
Comparison of Prior Studies to 1987 NAA Study

	NAA Study		McKelvey & Rogers[1] (1971)	Briggs & Anderson[2] (1980)	Petersen & Rezler[3] (1977)	King[4] (1971)
	NAA	Total				
Sample	NAA Arbitrators in U.S.	All Arbitrators in U.S.	NAA Arbitrators	AAA Arbitrators in Los Angeles and San Francisco	NAA and Non-NAA Arbitrators in Midwest	BNA Published Arbitrators
Size	358	262	222	133	97	134
Average Age	61.7	58.4	57	57.6	57.9	57.9
Percentages						
Law Degree	57.8	55.4	58.6[5]	45	59	68.9
Ph.D.	30.2	22.9	29.3	23	na	na
Affiliations						
AAA	81.3	60.1	na	na	na	64.9
IRRA	74.0	52.2	na	na	na	35.8
Full-time	40.8	16.4	25.2	na	32	na
Part-time	53.1	60.6	74.8	na	68	na
Inactive	6.1	22.9	na	na	na	na

Estimate for total population of arbitrators in United States based on weighted responses from both non-NAA arbitrators and NAA arbitrators. See above for weights.

[1] McKelvey and Rogers, "Survey of the Arbitration Profession in 1968," in Arbitration and the Public Interest, Proceedings of the 24th Annual Meeting of the National Academy of Arbitrators, eds. Barbara D. Dennis and Gerald G. Somers (Washington: BNA Books, 1971), p. 275.

[2] Briggs and Anderson, "An Empirical Investigation of Arbitrator Acceptability," Indus. Rel. 19 (1980), p. 163.

[3] Petersen and Rezler, "Fee Setting and Other Administrative Practices of Labor Arbitrators," LA 68 (1977), p. 1383.

[4] King, "Some Aspects of the Active Labor Arbitrator," Personnel J. (1971), p. 115.

[5] Computed by combining the holders of LL.B. (81) and J.D. (49) degrees and dividing by 222. McKelvey and Rogers, supra note 1, p. 282.

54 percent of the arbitrators in their population actually held law degrees. The NAA match on this variable is nearly perfect (57.8% for this study, and 58.6% for McKelvey and Rogers). The comparative figures on percentage of Ph.D. arbitrators are also almost identical.

The percentages of arbitrators affiliated with the AAA and the IRRA in this study diverge from the figures reported by King. But these differences may be explained by the sampling criteria King used. He considered only arbitrators with a minimum of five awards published in *Labor Arbitration Reports*. He may have drawn from a population of arbitrators that was systematically more experienced than those sampled in this study, particularly the non-NAA respondents.

The findings from this study on the percentages of full and part-time arbitrators differ from those found by Petersen and Rezler, and McKelvey and Rogers. This divergence probably comes from differences in survey questions. The current study first separated active and nonactive arbitrators and then asked active arbitrators whether they had worked full-time or part-time as arbitrators. McKelvey and Rogers offered the forced choice: Do you do labor arbitration (a) on a full-time basis or (b) part-time? Nonactive arbitrators most likely marked part-time, when they were not doing any arbitration. In the Petersen and Rezler study, respondents were reported to be "part-time" if they reported having another occupation or being retired. Petersen and Rezler did not ask if the respondents had served as an arbitrator during a recent time period. In fact, about 16 percent of their respondents who reported that they were working part-time were either retired (11.8 %) or did not indicate their other full-time occupation (4.4 %).

A Priori Comparisons

The last reason for inferring representativeness of the NAA study comes from a comparison of certain characteristics of the sample with known characteristics of the arbitration population. The lists supplied by the cooperating agencies enabled the Committee to determine precisely the NAA membership status and the geographic location of the respondents, and they provided almost certain information on gender (based on first names).

The characteristics of the sample were extremely close to these known characteristics of the populations. The membership distribution for the entire population of arbitrators is slightly different from that in the sample of responses (Table 1.3). But this was not surprising because the sample was admittedly somewhat over-representative of NAA members. The use of expansion weights described earlier in this chapter implicitly adjusts for this bias.

Table 1.4 presents data on gender for non-NAA and NAA arbitrators and suggests that representativeness on the basis of gender is present in the total sample. Although a similar table is not presented, Bognanno and Smith reached the same conclusion with respect to geographic location.[13]

In summary, the sample was relatively large and the sampling plan was constructed with representativeness in mind. The results on many variables matched up well with results from prior studies and with known characteristics of the population. All of these factors make it reasonable to assume that the sample of arbitrators in the NAA study is representative of the population and that it is appropriate to make inferences about the total population of arbitrators in the United States based upon this analysis.

Table 1.3
1987 Academy Membership: Adjusted Population and Sample

	(1) Adjusted Population	(2) Distribution of Adjusted Population (percentages)	(3) Adjusted Survey Response[1]	(4) Distribution of Responses (percentages)
NAA Arbitrators	592	17.0	358	23.4
Non-NAA Arbitrators	2,885	83.0	1,172	76.6
Total	3,477	100.0	1,530	100.0

[1] This count was estimated by assuming that the response rate for the 20% random sample of non-NAA arbitrators (40.62%) would have been maintained if 100% of non-NAA arbitrators had been surveyed. Using adjusted figures from Table 1.1, there were 2,885 non-NAA arbitrators in 1986. Twenty percent, or 702 bona fide arbitrators, were sampled, but 57 were "not eligible," leaving an adjusted sample size of 45. There were 262 usable returns for a 40.62% response rate.

Outline of the Book

Most of this chapter has been devoted to describing the nature of the study, its significance, methodology, and representativeness. The next chapter shifts attention to the nature of those who practice the arbitration profession. It reviews past studies of the backgrounds, experiences, aspirations, and careers of labor arbitrators and contrasts the findings from these studies with those of the NAA study. This chapter also examines the characteristics of a number of important arbitrator subpopulations.

The National Academy takes center stage in the third chapter. This chapter shows many of the differences between arbitrators who have been selected for NAA membership and those who have not. It tells something about the Academy and its standards for admission. Among other things, it answers questions about the differences between Academy and non-Academy arbitrators in terms of background, organizational memberships, employment status, caseloads, and fees.

Chapter 4 provides a systematic examination of the arbitration career. Because arbitration is often a second career, the author looks at the years prior to entry and the events that triggered interest in the field. He describes the years while the young arbitrator struggled for survival in the field, the years when the caseload reached a peak, and the years of decline. The chapter examines career aspirations and the kinds of training that arbitrators perceived as necessary for career development. The chapter closes with a model of career development.

Table 1.4
1987 Gender Distribution: Population and Subsamples

	(1) Population[1]	(2) Distribution of Population (percentages)	(3) Survey Responses	(4) Distribution of Responses (percentages)
NAA Arbitrators[2]				
Males	587	95.6	345	96.4
Females	27	4.4	13	3.6
Non-NAA Arbitrators[2]				
Males	3,261	92.8	238	90.8
Females	252	7.2	24	9.2
Total Arbitrators				
Males	3,848	93.2	583	91.8[3]
Females	279	6.8	37	8.2[3]

[1] Where gender could not be determined (individuals were classified on the basis of their first names), the "unclear" individuals were proportionately classified as males and females.

[2] The chi-square difference between means or proportions for NAA arbitrators and non-NAA arbitrators based on sex is statistically significant at the $p = .004$ level.

[3] Data representing all arbitrators are based on estimates regarding the total population of arbitrators after applying the expansion weights (1.6536 for NAA members and 11.0114 for non-NAA arbitrators).

The fifth chapter focuses on cases. This chapter investigates how many cases arbitrators have, where they come from, and the issues involved. It also examines the variables that are related to caseload differences among arbitrators, the effects of NAA membership upon cases, and caseload development patterns of different kinds of arbitrators.

Economic concerns are the topic of Chapter 6. Earnings from the practice of arbitration depend on the number of decisions handed down and charges per case. Arbitrators charge different kinds of fees—in addition to charges for conducting hearings, they charge for study and drafting time, for untimely cancellations, travel, executive sessions, and sometimes, docketing fees. This chapter examines how much arbitrators make, the sources and the composition of their earnings, and it comes to some interesting conclusions about the earnings of male and female arbitrators.

In the seventh chapter, attention shifts to whether there are shortages or surpluses of arbitration services and arbitrators, including a review of the geographic aspect to this question. This chapter's exploration also sheds light on why arbitrators and the parties proffer opposite answers to this question. The final chapter provides a summary of the material that the book has covered, draws some overall conclusions about the practice and profession of arbitration today, and looks into the future.

Labor Arbitration as a Profession

Is arbitration a profession? There is no doubt in the minds of most arbitrators that they belong to a profession.[14] The concept of a profession, however, is very complex. It takes more to be a professional than a simple claim that you are one. The groundwork studies in this area have concluded that most professions are marked by the following characteristics.[15]

Specialized Skill and Training

A profession is supposed to be based upon some underlying body of theory, and its knowledge base is presumed to be highly specialized. People enter most professions only after a long and rigorous period of academic training. Baseball players and plumbers may call themselves professional, but would not qualify under this definition.

As a group, arbitrators are well educated and have extensive work experience. They know about industrial relations and the practical and legal aspects of collective bargaining. They have developed highly specialized skills in listening to both sides of a dispute; in not allowing personal prejudice to influence a decision; and in communicating their decision through well-written awards. Nevertheless, it may be argued that an arbitrator does not possess the systematic knowledge base found in the four "classic" professions: law, medicine, teaching, and the ministry.

Control Over Fees or Salaries

Traditionally, people have drawn connections between status and income, and in the effort to improve status, professionals and their associations tend to pay attention to compensation. Some recognized professions, such as medicine, exert influence over the fees charged by members. But others, notably teaching and the ministry, have much less influence.

Individual arbitrators set their own fees, and there are no public regulations or professional association rules affecting either entry into the field or pay practices. For some, the practice of arbitration provides a comfortable second income, while others maintain a successful full-time practice. But there are many practitioners with quite small practices and modest incomes (see Chapter 6).

Formation of a Professional Association

All of the recognized professions and most of the occupations claiming to be professions have established associations for their members. A professional association fulfills many functions. It provides an opportunity for members to meet, exchange ideas, and get to know one another. A professional association also performs an educational function and, through the process of socializing its members, develops member group identity and a sense of commitment. Professional associations also provide forums for discussions of topics that are of concern to members; they represent the profession to the outside world; perform a public relations function; and they may lobby legislative bodies.

In 1947 a small group of arbitrators met to discuss the advisability of establishing a professional association of individuals engaged in the arbitration of labor disputes.[16] This meeting led to the establishment of the National Academy of Arbitrators in September of that year. The NAA now provides all of the functions normally associated with a typical professional association. Article II, Section 1 of the NAA Constitution (as amended April 29, 1975) states that:

The purposes for which the Academy is formed are: To establish and foster the highest standards of integrity, competence, honor, and character among those engaged in the arbitration of labor-management disputes on a professional basis; to secure the acceptance of and adherence to the Code of Professional Responsibility for Arbitrators of Labor-Management Disputes . . . ; to promote the study and understanding of the arbitration of labor-management disputes; to encourage friendly association among the members of the profession; to cooperate with other organizations, institutions and learned societies interested in labor-management relations, and to do any and all things which shall be appropriate in the furtherance of these purposes.

A Code of Ethics

One of the normal products of a professional society is a code of ethics that governs professional practice. The code provides a basis for enforcing rules and standards of conduct. Through persuasion and the threat of ouster, the code helps the membership maintain a high level of ethical conduct.

One of the committees formed at that first meeting of the NAA was the Ethics Committee. This Committee, now called the Committee on Professional Responsibility and Grievances, monitors NAA member practices, assuring that they meet the Code of Professional Responsibility in their practice as arbitrators. Finally, a "Code of Professional Responsibility for Arbitrators of Labor-Management Disputes" has been jointly developed and promulgated by the American Arbitration Association, the

National Academy of Arbitrators, and the Federal Mediation and Conciliation Service. State agencies and the National Mediation Board have also endorsed the Code.

Professional Authority, Sanctions, and Licensing

Because a profession is built upon a claim to specialized knowledge, members of the profession typically hold that they alone can prescribe for the client and evaluate how well or how poorly a member of the profession has performed. The presence of a code of conduct lends credence to the professional's desire for self-regulation. The existence of a functioning association allows the professional to claim that the association is best equipped to exercise this authority.

All of these considerations provide a basis for licensing. The profession licenses its own and the community accepts its authority to do so. Most professional associations go through a long period of political agitation to obtain from public authorities the right to license prospective members. This licensing power, in turn, allows the association to control entry into the profession.

The NAA does not control entry into the field. There is no licensing of arbitrators and, for that matter, there are no provisions for lesser requirements, such as certification or registration. Entry into arbitration is controlled by the clients who use the services. The professional arbitrator must pass the test of acceptability by the parties. In labor arbitration, this is the ultimate test. Arbitrators who are not professional in handling the duties and responsibilities of the position will not be selected in the future by the parties. But the NAA does bestow a sign of recognition on those arbitrators whom the clients themselves have utilized and accepted over a number of years. The NAA establishes criteria for acceptance into the Academy, and one of its important committees is the Membership Committee, which reviews the credentials of those who apply. The membership itself votes for the admission of newcomers. But the punitive powers of the NAA are not strong, and while members may be cautioned, sanctioned, or even dismissed from the Academy, such action may have little or no effect on the individual's caseload.

Is arbitration a profession? Arbitration does not possess all of the classic requirements of a profession: for example, there is no licensing requirement and the sanctioning powers of the NAA are quite limited. On the other hand, the people who practice in this field possess similar and unique skills, have comparable and extensive knowledge, go through a long period of (pre-entry) training, possess conceptually based rules of practices and procedures that are normally identified with the term "professional," and share a common code of ethical conduct. On balance, arbitrators meet so many of the traditional requirements of professionalism that they can rightly be considered to be professional.

Summary and Conclusions

The purpose of this opening chapter is to establish the foundations for the book that follows. The book, as a whole, examines the contemporary practice and profession of arbitration in the United States. It tells an untold story about who arbitrators are and what they do. This chapter provided some background on the NAA study, set forth some of the anticipated contributions of the book, described the design of the study and the methodology employed, and showed why one can, with a great deal of confidence, conclude that the material between the covers of this book is, in fact, an accurate portrayal of the field. The chapter closed with a discussion of whether or not arbitration is a profession.

Notes

1. Howard G. Foster, Editor-in-Chief, *An Annotated Bibliography of Labor Arbitration, Labor Arbitration* no. 1308 (January 20, 1986).
2. Mario F. Bognanno and Clifford E. Smith, "The Demographic and Professional Characteristics of Arbitrators in North America," in *Arbitration 1988: Emerging Issues for the 1990s*, Proceedings of the 41st Annual Meeting of the National Academy of Arbitrators, ed. Gladys W. Gruenberg (Washington: BNA Books, Inc., 1989), pp. 266–289.
3. Stephen Hawking, *A Brief History of Time* (Toronto: Bantam Books, 1988).
4. Frank Elkouri and Edna Asper Elkouri, *How Arbitration Works*, 4th ed. (Washington: BNA Books, Inc., 1985), p. 2.
5. Edwin E. Witte, "The Future of Labor Arbitration: A Challenge," in *The Profession of Labor Arbitration: Selected Papers from the First Seven Annual Meetings of the National Academy of Arbitrators*, ed. Jean T. McKelvey (Washington: BNA Books, Inc., 1957), p. 4.
6. Elkouri and Elkouri, p. 13.
7. J. Joseph Loewenberg, "The Structure of Grievance Procedures in the U.S. Postal Service," *Labor Law Journal* 35 (1985), pp. 44–51.
8. Charles J. Coleman, *Managing Labor Relations in the Public Sector* (San Francisco: Jossey-Bass, Inc., 1990), pp. 142–144.
9. Courtney D. Gifford, *Directory of United States Labor Arbitrators* (Washington: BNA Books, Inc., 1985).
10. The original mailing was sent to a number of Canadian agencies. The responses from these agencies indicated the presence of 31 Canadian arbitrators who were members of the NAA and 199 who were not. But only 27 Canadian arbitrators later responded to the questionnaire and only 16 were from the non-NAA group (8.0%). This number was too small to be judged representative of the

total population of arbitrators in Canada and to provide suitable statistics for generalizing about the Canadian practice of arbitration. With some reluctance, the Committee decided to eliminate the Canadian responses and to focus only on the practice and profession of arbitrators residing in the United States.

11. The names of arbitrators within a given zip code were listed alphabetically. Then a random number between one and five was drawn and the number was three. The process began with the third name within the first zip code on the list, and thereafter every fifth name throughout the remainder of the list was selected.

12. Most of the analysis in this book, however, deals only with those arbitrators who were in active practice in 1986. This criterion eliminated 91 respondents from the data set (14.7% of the sample). See Chapter 2 for more information on these "Uncalled Arbitrators."

13. Bognanno and Smith, pp. 266–289.

14. Ralph T. Seward, "Report of the Special Committee on Professionalism," in *Arbitration 1987: The Academy at Forty*, Proceedings of the 40th Annual Meeting of the National Academy of Arbitrators, ed. Gladys W. Gruenberg (Washington: BNA Books, Inc., 1988), p. 221.

15. The following material on professionalism is based on A. M. Carr-Saunders, *The Professions* (Oxford: Clarendon Press, 1933); Ernest Greenwood, "Attributes of a Profession," *Social Work* 2, no. 3 (July 1957), pp. 44–55; Everett C. Hughes, "The Professions in Society," *The Canadian Journal of Economics and Political Science* 26, no. 1 (Feb. 1960), pp. 54–61; Howard M. Vollmer and Donald L. Mills, *Professionalization* (Englewood Cliffs, N.J.: Prentice-Hall, Inc., 1966); and Steven Briggs in Gladys W. Gruenberg, ed., pp. 263–269.

16. Charles C. Killingsworth, "Twenty-five Years of Labor Arbitration and the Future," in *Labor Arbitration at the Quarter-Century Mark*, Proceedings of the 25th Annual Meeting of the National Academy of Arbitrators, ed. Barbara D. Dennis (Washington: BNA Books, Inc., 1973), p. 28.

2

The Varied Portraits of the Labor Arbitrator

Charles J. Coleman and Perry A. Zirkel

Introduction

With this chapter, the attention of the book shifts from the profession of arbitration to the characteristics of the people who practice it. Much of the information in this chapter provides a foundation for several chapters that follow, particularly those that examine the differences between arbitrators who have been elected to the National Academy of Arbitrators (NAA) and those who have not, entry into the field, and the arbitrator's caseload, career, and earnings.

Almost from the time that the first award was issued, questions have been raised about the nature of the people who practice the profession of arbitration—their education, how they came to be arbitrators, their attitudes, caseloads, and earnings. This chapter uses the information gathered in the study sponsored by the NAA as a basis for answering questions about the people who practice labor arbitration today.

This chapter has three objectives. The first is to describe the characteristics of today's labor arbitrators' backgrounds, experiences, and aspirations, and the second is to determine whether those characteristics differ from the ones reported in earlier studies. To accomplish these objectives, the chapter sketches the portrait of the arbitrator that has come from past studies and then contrasts that portrait with the one that emerges from the NAA study.

The third objective is to produce a number of fairly specific insights into the nature and the activities of the people who practice this profession.

We accomplish this objective by painting a number of smaller portraits or "miniatures." Each miniature is drawn from a subset of survey respondents that was selected to provide a more refined set of insights into the arbitrators themselves, their activity levels, and the changing nature of the profession. These smaller sketches highlight the differences between oldtimers and newcomers to the field, the characteristics of the very busy, "mainline" arbitrators, the features of arbitrators who emphasize public sector work, the attributes of those who most desperately want to expand their practice, the characteristics of women and minority arbitrators and of those who get no cases at all. The overall goal of the chapter is to produce a set of generalizable results that fill holes left by previous research, resolve contradictions in the literature, and provide a comprehensive picture of today's arbitrators and at least some of the forces that shape their careers.[1]

The Older Portrait: The Past Studies

Two kinds of studies have provided insight into the backgrounds of labor arbitrators, their experiences, and their aspirations. One kind, called *partial* studies in this chapter, typically provide information on a few selected characteristics of arbitrators (most often age, education, or caseload), often gathered in the course of studying something else. The second kind, termed *comprehensive*, consists of studies that consciously set out to provide a reasonably complete description of the arbitrators' attitudes, background, and career. Although the NAA is not the only source, it is the richest source of the comprehensive studies.

The Partial Studies

The earliest study that came to our attention was the 1951 survey of a "national cross section" of almost 2,000 management and union representatives and arbitrators. This study, performed by Edgar L. Warren and Irving Bernstein, focused on the scope of arbitration and hearing procedures, but it also reported that the respondents had heard an average of four interest cases and 32 grievances over the previous two years. The authors also described arbitrators as striving professionals, "eager to elevate their status," wanting to broaden the scope of arbitration, practice it full-time, and charge higher fees.[2]

Some years later Robert Coulson provided information on age and occupational status. In his 1965 study of 370 arbitrators who decided one or more American Arbitration Association cases the previous year, he found that the typical arbitrator was between 50 and 60 years of age. More than 40 percent had a full-time position in higher education, about 30 percent were attorneys, and 15 percent were full-time arbitrators.[3]

In 1972, James F. Power provided information on the education and work experience of about 130 successful applicants for the FMCS arbitration roster. Their median age was less than 50. Almost one-quarter had master's degrees and 10 percent had doctorates. One in four were full-time arbitrators, a similar number were college professors, and almost 40 percent were attorneys.[4]

The next year Donald J. Petersen and Julius Rezler reported the results of their survey of 85 randomly selected members of the NAA and 113 nonmembers listed with the AAA's Midwest Region. They focused on billing and administrative procedures but also found that the average age of arbitrators was almost 60. Over half had law degrees and half of these were still practicing law. Almost one-third practiced arbitration on a full-time basis, while approximately one-quarter had an academic base.[5]

In a 1980 survey of 133 arbitrators from the Los Angeles and San Francisco panels of the American Arbitration Association, Steven Briggs and John C. Anderson also reported an average age close to 60. Almost half the respondents had degrees in law and roughly one-quarter were Ph.D.'s.[6] Perry Zirkel's 1983 study of 396 AAA cases was primarily concerned with the characteristics of awards rather than arbitrators. But he reported that 93.4 percent of the arbitrators were men and that two-thirds of their cases came from the private sector.[7]

The More Comprehensive Studies

Table 2.1 summarizes the results of five fairly comprehensive non-NAA studies of the backgrounds and careers of arbitrators. Brian L. King's 1971 study was based on 134 arbitrators who had published five or more awards in Volumes 41–50 of the Bureau of National Affairs *Labor Arbitration Reports* (1963 to 1968).[8] His data were derived from the capsule biographies published in the Index to each volume. Herbert G. Heneman and Marcus H. Sandver followed King's approach but used Volumes 61–70 of the same source and reported on 250 arbitrators with four or more awards.[9]

John Herrick's studies were based upon a survey of more than 500 arbitrators on the FMCS roster,[10] and the paper by J. Timothy Sprehe and Jeffrey Small, based upon a survey of more than 1,000 arbitrators, concentrated on the differences between NAA and non-NAA arbitrators.[11] The analysis performed by A. Dale Allen and Daniel F. Jennings was based upon a survey of 296 NAA members.[12] The NAA periodically studies its own membership. Table 2.2 offers an overview of the results that are germane to this paper from seven NAA surveys conducted between 1952 and 1982.[13]

Table 2.1
Comprehensive Non-Academy Studies of Labor Arbitrators

Study	King, 1971	Heneman & Sandver, 1983	Herrick, 1983	Sprehe & Small 1984	Allen & Jennings 1987
Average Age	57.9 yrs.	60.1	58.7	58.0	62.0
Percent Male		98.0%	98.2%	95.3%	
Academic Training					
Law	68.9%		51.0%	54.3%	51%
Economics	14.5%		25.0%		
Business	7.6%				
Highest Degree					
Law	68.9%	72.4%			30%
Ph.D.		18.4%			
No Degree					10%
Occupation					
Attorney	38.8%	38.4%	30.0%		46%
Academic	37.3%	31.6%	25.0%		36%
Full-Time Arbitrator	21.5%		24.8%	22.8%	
Previous Experience					
Government	72.4%				
Management	15.7%				27%
Education	13.4%				
Union	2.2%				8%
Management and Union					30%
None	20.2%				
Affiliations					
AAA	64.9%	76.0%			92% AAA & FMCS combined
FMCS	50.8%	65.6%			
NAA	64.1%	46.8%			100%
IRRA	35.8%				67%
SPIDR					48%
Permanent Umpireship	34.3%			45.9%	
Average Experience		30.9 yrs.	14.2 yrs.	10 yrs.	21.2 yrs.
Average Annual Caseload			35.9	17	62.5

The Portrait Drawn in the Older Studies

For the most part, these older studies represent the first stages of analysis of the practice and profession of arbitration. They are typically descriptive in nature. Most of them provide simple portrayals of arbitrators and their practices, using such fundamental descriptive statistics as ranges, means, and medians. But they have rarely produced much insight

Table 2.2
Academy Studies of Labor Arbitrators

Year	1952	1957	1962	1964	1969	1972	1982
Respondents	115	89	174	98	222	227	391
Average Age	49.7		52.7		57.0		59.2
Education							
No College Degree	4%	1%	2%		1%		
Bachelor's	2%	3%					
Master's	4%	10%					
Ph.D.	41%	46%	50%		58%		
Law	41%	35%	38%		29%		
Academic Training							
Law			46%		55%		58%
Economics			39%		34%		28%
Affiliations							
AAA							12%
IRRA							66%
SPIDR							43%
Occupation							
Academic	59%	62%	42%		45%		29%
Attorney	22%	26%	10%		17%		13%
Full-Time Arbitrator	7%	2%	33%		25%	38%	46%
Permanent Umpireship	51%	36%	59%		68%		
Average Experience	11.2 yrs.				19.6 yrs.		
Average Annual Caseload	35.7	30.3	40.0	40.1	37.0	54.1	

into one of the topics that is important to this chapter—the relationship between the life of the arbitrator and his or her career.[14]

Many of the studies, furthermore, labored with small or narrow samples, or low response rates. Because their samples were not representative of the arbitrator population, it is not surprising that many of the findings were inconsistent. The inconsistency is clearly evident in the comprehensive non-NAA studies (for example, in the results concerning years of experience and caseload). The findings that do carry over from one study to another usually relate to areas where there is little variation among arbitrators (for example, race or sex). In at least two cases (King and Heneman-Sandver), the methodology eliminated all but highly experienced arbitrators. Finally, while the NAA papers are the most consistent and provide the sweep of history, they are limited because they study only one segment of the population—Academy members.

Despite their shortcomings, however, the early studies provide valuable baseline information. They showed that:

(1) Arbitrators are predominantly male. The non-Academy studies showed that more than 90 percent of arbitrators were men.

(2) They are elderly and may be getting more so. Both NAA and non-NAA studies reported that arbitrators were in their late fifties or early sixties. The NAA studies also showed that the average age increased by a decade between 1952 and 1982.

(3) They are well educated but come from widely differing educational backgrounds. More than half of the NAA members have graduate training in law and a similar proportion have Ph.D.'s. The educational level of non-NAA arbitrators seems to be slightly lower.

(4) Almost all came into arbitration from another job. King, for example, determined that 72 percent of his sample came from government.

(5) A large number of them join associations related to the field of labor relations.

(6) Most work at the profession part-time, with their primary occupation being either law or teaching.

(7) Many earn very little from arbitration and the ones who earn the most tend to belong to the Academy. The average caseload for Academy members reported by the 1982 NAA study and by Allen and Jennings in 1987 was over fifty.

The Portrait from the NAA Study

The general portrait drawn of the arbitrator in this chapter is based upon Tables 2.3 through 2.6. These tables provide the results from the NAA study on the same kinds of background variables, association memberships, career elements, and caseload aspirations that the earlier studies highlighted. The data reported in the tables apply only to active arbitrators—those who decided at least one case in 1986. The percentages, means, and medians in the tables were weighted according to the values described in Chapter 1 (1.6536 for NAA arbitrators and 11.0114 for non-NAA arbitrators). The figures below each percentage, mean, or median represent the number of respondents.

In these tables the data are broken down on the basis of full and part-time arbitrators. In 1986, roughly one in five active arbitrators practiced on a full-time basis. As Holley will report in the next chapter, 43.5 percent

Table 2.3a
Characteristics of Full-Time and Part-Time
U.S. Arbitrators' Demographics: Age, Race, Locale (1987)

Characteristics	Full-Time	Part-Time	All
Average Age	57.2 (n = 175)	56.7 (n = 351)	56.8 (n = 526)
		(percentages)	
Males*	81.9 (n = 159 men, 16 women)	93.5 (n = 338 men, 16 women)	91.0 (n = 497 men, 32 women)
White, non-hispanic	98.0 (n = 173)	96.6 (n = 343)	96.9 (n = 516)
Location** Four States with highest concentration of arbitrators	40.9 (n = 71)	32.2 (n = 111)	34.8 (n = 182)
Eight States with moderate concentration	36.4 (n = 62)	30.7 (n = 113)	31.9 (n = 175)
38 States with lowest concentration	14.0 (n = 34)	36.11 (n = 124)	33.3 (n = 158)

The following applies to all of Table 2.3 (sections a through f):

*p ≤ .05
**p ≤ .01
***p ≤ .001
X(p) ≤ .01 in weighted population but ns in unweighted survey group

Percentages, means, and medians have been drawn from the weighted population, but the figures in parentheses represent the number of actual respondents.

of the NAA members and 15 percent of the non-NAA arbitrators had full-time practices.

Age, Gender, Race, and Location

Confirming previous studies, arbitrators who were active in 1987 were elderly, white, non-hispanic men (Table 2.3a). The typical arbitrator was 57 years old and all but 3 percent were white and non-hispanic. Only 9 percent were women, but the percentage of women in the full-time ranks (18%) was almost three times as high as the percentage of women among the part-time arbitrators (6.5%). While only one-third of the men classified themselves as full-time arbitrators, half of the women did so.

Roughly two-thirds of the active arbitrators were located in twelve industrialized states where the union movement is comparatively strong. The primary offices of about one-third of the arbitration population were in California, Michigan, New York, and Pennsylvania, and an additional 30 percent were in Florida, Illinois, Massachusetts, Missouri, New Jersey, Ohio, Texas, and Wisconsin.

Full-time arbitrators were significantly more likely to establish offices in these twelve states, while part-timers were more likely to be found in the remaining areas. As will be developed more fully in the seventh chapter, arbitrators "fish where the fishing is good." Full-timers tend to practice in the states most likely to support full-time practices—the highly unionized, more industrialized states. The part-timer dominates in less unionized, less industrialized areas, where the lighter caseload fits with a part-time practice.

Education

There were some marginal differences between the two classes of active arbitrators with regard to undergraduate training (Table 2.3b). The most popular undergraduate major for the full-time arbitrators and the entire study group was liberal arts. The first choice of the part-time arbitrator and the second choice for the entire set was economics, political science, or government.

But highly significant differences existed between the groups in regard to postgraduate studies. Arbitrators invariably had undergraduate degrees and most had advanced degrees. Over half were attorneys, roughly one-quarter had master's degrees, and an equivalent percentage had doctorates. There was no difference between full and part-timers in regard to the law degree. But active full-time arbitrators who were not attorneys were much more likely to have stopped their education with a master's degree, and part-timers were considerably more likely to have a doctorate. All but 30 of the 146 responding Ph.D.'s arbitrated part-time, and, on a weighted basis, the percentage of doctorates among active part-time arbitrators nearly doubled the percentage in the full-time ranks.

Pre-Arbitration Work Experience

As Krislov shows more fully in Chapter 4, arbitration is seldom a first career (Table 2.3c). Today's arbitrators invariably began their work career in another capacity. At some time they came in contact with arbitration, liked what they saw, and moved into it, either on a part-time or full-time basis. Almost all of the survey respondents reported that arbitration was a second career and, for more than 60 percent, their job immediately prior to entering arbitration was in law, teaching, or industrial relations/human resources (IR/HR). Consistent with the possession of the doctorate noted

Table 2.3b
Educational Background (1987)

Four Chief Undergraduate Fields (X)	(percentages)		
	Full-Time	Part-Time	All
Admin.-IR/HR	32.2 (n = 36)	19.6 (n = 65)	22.3 (n = 101)
Business	5.6 (n = 16)	12.4 (n = 34)	10.9 (n = 50)
Economics, Political Science, Government	16.9 (n = 43)	27.6 (n = 98)	25.3 (n = 141)
Liberal Arts	33.8 (n = 35)	25.2 (n = 61)	27.0 (n = 96)
Degree Status			
No Degree	4.5 (n = 4)	1.6 (n = 4)	2.2 (n = 8)
Bachelor's[a]	39.2 (n = 65)	35.4 (n = 120)	36.2 (n = 185)
Master's***	31.2 (n = 53)	19.7 (n = 71)	22.1 (n = 126)
Ph.D.***	13.9 (n = 30)	27.1 (n = 116)	24.4 (n = 146)
Other[b]	11.2 (n = 21)	16.2 (n = 43)	15.1 (n = 64)
Total	100 (n = 175)	100 (n = 354)	100 (n = 529)

[a] including respondents listing "some graduate work: but no graduate degree."
[b] "no degree other than law" and non-respondents.

*p ≤ .05
**p ≤ .01
***p ≤ .001
X(p) ≤ .01 in weighted population but ns in unweighted survey group

Percentages, means, and medians have been drawn from the weighted population, but the figures in parentheses represent the number of actual respondents.

above, over one-third of the active part-time arbitrators reported that they were or had been members of the professoriate. The practice of law or IR/HR was the leading pre-arbitration occupation for the full-time respondents.

Many of the active arbitrators had held either a full-time IR/HR or union position sometime in their career. This tendency was much more

Table 2.3c
Pre-Arbitration Work Experience, Principal Pre-Arbitration Occupation
(1987*)**

	(percentages)		
Occupation	Full-Time	Part-Time	All
Law	25.7 (n = 59)	32.8 (n = 103)	31.3 (n = 162)
Teaching	14.5 (n = 38)	33.3 (n = 155)	29.4 (n = 193)
Management, IR/HR	21.9 (n = 29)	16.5 (n = 47)	17.6 (n = 76)
Neutral	27.5 (n = 31)	9.2 (n = 27)	13.0 (n = 58)
Other	10.3 (n = 18)	8.3 (n = 22)	8.8 (n = 40)

Full-Time Work in Human Resources, Prior to Arbitration			
	(percentages)		
	Full-Time	Part-Time	All
Full-Time Union Position (X)	15.4 (n = 18)	8.8 (n = 30)	10.0 (n = 48)
Full-Time IR/HR Position (X)	44.0 (n = 57)	30.4 (n = 98)	33.3 (n = 155)

*p ≤ .05
**p ≤ .01
***p ≤ .001
X(p) ≤ .01 in weighted population but ns in unweighted survey group

Percentages, means, and medians have been drawn from the weighted population, but the figures in parentheses represent the number of actual respondents.

pronounced among the full-time arbitrators. Over 40 percent of the full-timers had worked in IR/HR, and an additional 15 percent had been union employees, as opposed to 30 percent IR/HR and 8 percent union for the part-timers.

Associations

Working arbitrators in 1987 were active in professional associations concerned with labor relations or labor law (Table 2.3d). But some of the most consistent and telling differences between full and part-time arbitrators concerned their membership in such societies and their focus.

Table 2.3d
Membership in Professional Organizations (1987)

Organization	(percentages)		
	Full Time	Part Time	All
AAA***	88.6	64.3	69.5
	(n = 158)	(n = 249)	(n = 407)
IRRA**	73.9	54.7	58.8
	(n = 131)	(n = 223)	(n = 354)
SPIDR***	60.3	38.8	43.4
	(n = 102)	(n = 148)	(n = 250)
FLRP***	17.3	1.6	4.9
	(n = 30)	(n = 14)	(n = 44)
Labor Law Section	40.6	34.5	35.8
of Regional Bar*	(n = 75)	(n = 114)	(n = 189)
ABA	20.1	20.4	20.3
	(n = 45)	(n = 85)	(n = 130)
NAA***	43.1	14.8	20.7
	(n = 146)	(n = 190)	(n = 336)
No other organizations***	73.7	47.3	52.8
	(n = 124)	(n = 187)	(n = 311)

*p ≤ .05
**p ≤ .01
***p ≤ .001
X(p) ≤ .01 in weighted population but ns in unweighted survey group

Percentages, means, and medians have been drawn from the weighted population, but the figures in parentheses represent the number of actual respondents.

A far greater proportion of the full-time arbitrators belonged to almost all of the professional organizations listed in the study. But those arbitrators also refrained from joining societies outside the labor relations field. Only one-quarter of the full-time active arbitrators listed membership in another organization as opposed to almost half of the part-timers. The data suggest that full-time arbitrators focus in a more concentrated way on activities somehow related to arbitration. Part-time arbitrators tend to extend their activities more widely, which is not surprising among a group of people who have interests other than arbitration.

Experiences and Cases

The arbitrators active in 1986 were well-experienced (Table 2.3e). On average, they had worked in this field for twenty years. While there were

Table 2.3e
Career Related Variables (1986)

Characteristic (mean except when otherwise noted)	Full-Time	Part-Time	All
Years in arbitration	22.9 (n = 170)	19.8 (n = 352)	20.2 (n = 522)
Cases in career			
Range	3-8,000	1-6,000	1-8,000
Mean***	857	210	343
Median	400	75	114
	(n = 167)	(n = 348)	(n = 515)
Grievances in 1986			
Range	3-404	1-180	1-404
Mean***	64.5	13.7	24.4
Median	50	7	10
	(n = 174)	(n = 350)	(n = 524)
Interest Cases in 1986			
Range	0-26	0-20	0-26
Mean***	5.5	2.8	3.7
Median (for those who	3	2	2
heard at least one case)	(n = 97)	(n = 103)	(n = 200)
Caseload from private sector (X)	62.4% (n = 168)	55.0% (n = 311)	56.5% (n = 479)
Caseload from public sector**	37.6% (n = 162)	45.0% (n = 291)	43.5% (n = 453)
Part-time only Income from arbitration		21.6% (n = 346)	
Days per month on arbitration		4.1 (n = 335)	

*p ≤ .05
**p ≤ .01
***p ≤ .001
X(p) ≤ .01 in weighted population but ns in unweighted survey group

Percentages, means, and medians have been drawn from the weighted population, but the figures in parentheses represent the number of actual respondents.

no statistically significant differences between full and part-time arbitrators in this regard, there were highly significant caseload differences.

The distribution of career cases for both full and part-time arbitrators was skewed. A small percentage of the active arbitrators were extremely busy. A few full-time arbitrators reported that they had decided 8,000 cases and the busiest part-timer reported 6,000. Sixty respondents (representing some 13% of the sample) indicated that they had decided 2,000 or more cases in their careers. Figures like these raise the means greatly and suggest that the medians on Table 2.3e provide a more representative picture of caseloads.

Full-time arbitrators who were active in 1986 had, up to that point in their careers, decided a mean of about 850 and a median of 400 cases while part-timers had heard a mean of 210 and a median of 75. It is important to remember that these careers were still in process: none had completed their career in arbitration and many had hardly begun. For arbitrators much further advanced in their careers (a minimum of thirty years of experience), the respective means and medians for career cases were 1,600 and 1,200. These figures were almost six times the mean number of career cases for arbitrators with less than thirty years' experience (272 cases) and twelve times the median (100 cases).

In 1986, the busiest full-time arbitrator heard over 400 cases. The mean for full-timers was 65 cases and the median was 50. The mean number of cases heard by part-time arbitrators was 14 and the median was 7, although one person listing himself as part-time reported 180 cases!

Because interest arbitration is a public sector phenomenon and many states have not passed interest arbitration laws, not all arbitrators hear interest cases.[15] Only 45 percent of the active full-time arbitrators and 30 percent of the active part-timers heard any interest cases at all in 1986. Considering only those arbitrators who reported one or more interest cases, the mean for full-timers was about five cases and the median was three. For part-timers, the mean was three and the median, two interest cases.

There was a small difference between full and part-time arbitrators in the percentage of 1986 cases that came from the private sector (62% for active full-time arbitrators and 55% for part-time). In 1986, active part-time arbitrators typically made about 20 percent of their income from arbitration and spent four days a month at it.

Caseload Aspirations

Two questions provided some insight into arbitrators' feelings about their caseloads (Table 2.3f). One question, posed only to the part-time arbitrators, was: "Do you want to practice full-time?" The other was asked of all active respondents: "Please explain why you would like more or less cases in the future." The responses "need less funds," "want to slow down," or "be more selective," were interpreted as showing a desire to reduce caseload; "want the same number" and "comfortable work load," as signifying contentment with the existing number of cases; and

Table 2.3f
Career Orientations of Arbitrators (1986)

	(percentages)		
Desired Change in Caseload**	Full-Time	Part-Time	All
Increase caseload	38.0 (n = 29)	49.5 (n = 104)	47.0 (n = 133)
Keep caseload about the same	32.6 (n = 38)	26.7 (n = 73)	28.0 (n = 111)
Decrease caseload	29.4 (n = 38)	23.7 (n = 85)	25.0 (n = 143)
Part-time arbitrators aspiring to full-time status		39.3 (n = 114)	

$^*p \le .05$
$^{**}p \le .01$
$^{***}p \le .001$
$X(p) \le .01$ in weighted population but ns in unweighted survey group

Percentages, means, and medians have been drawn from the weighted population, but the figures in parentheses represent the number of actual respondents.

the responses "more income," "can do more," and "like to keep busy" were thought to signify a desire for more cases.

Almost half of the active arbitrators wanted to expand their caseload. The part-timers expressed the strongest desire for an increase. Half of the part-time active arbitrators, as opposed to 38 percent of full-timers, wanted a larger caseload. Forty percent of the part-time arbitrators wanted to practice full-time.

The Miniature Portraits

This section of the chapter expands the information portrayed thus far by sketching some of the features of six subgroups of arbitrators. The first sketch focuses upon age and experience and addresses the question of change in the characteristics of the people who practice arbitration. The second picture spotlights the characteristics of the busiest members of the profession, called the "mainline" arbitrators. The third picture focuses on some of the differences between arbitrators with a public sector emphasis in their practice and those who stress the private sector. The fourth portrait deals with the characteristics of arbitrators who want to expand their practices.

The last two sketches call attention to potential problem areas in the field. Arbitration is and has been a profession dominated by white men, and many observers have argued that the field needs new blood. Because the issue of a potential shortage of arbitrators periodically surfaces, the fifth sketch, therefore, focuses on the women and minorities who have come into this field, and the last one highlights the arbitrators who want cases but get none.

Oldtimers and Newcomers

Arbitrators remain busy until very late in their careers. Arbitrators with thirty or more years of experience heard a mean of thirty cases and a median of twenty in 1986. The more experienced arbitrators also tended to refuse more cases, to report that their schedules were full, and the more experienced part-time arbitrators made a greater proportion of their income from arbitration. Building on experience and past contacts, the senior group received more cases through panel memberships and direct selection. As expected, there was a highly significant positive relationship between experience and NAA membership. But the strong relationship between years of arbitration experience and grievance caseload was not reflected in the interest arbitration caseload. The number of interest arbitration cases of the less experienced arbitrators was not materially different from the number decided by the more experienced ones.

When the arbitration population was broken down into groups with similar ages and levels of experience, it became clear that the people who came into the field many years ago differed from their younger colleagues in education and in gender. The more experienced arbitrators were more likely to have undergraduate degrees in economics, government, or political science, while the less senior ones tended to have had undergraduate training in liberal arts. The older arbitrators also had a more academically oriented education, and they were more tied into universities: the largest group of Ph.D.'s came from their ranks, and a large number had taught in the past or were teaching in 1986. Younger arbitrators were more likely to have trained and worked in law.

Finally, almost all of the women were in the younger group. For example, of the 87 respondents who had logged thirty years or more arbitration experience, only one was a woman. This person represented less than 1 percent of the population of female arbitrators.

The Mainline Arbitrator

In this chapter the term *mainline* refers to arbitrators who are well established and have heard the largest number of cases. In operationalizing this concept, the first step was to reduce the study group to arbitrators who were well established in the profession (see Table 2.4). The

Table 2.4
Caseload Characteristics of Mainline (ML) and Non-Mainline (NML) Arbitrators (1986)

	Mean Number			
	Full-Time		Part-Time	
	ML	NML	ML	NML
Career Grievance Cases	2,241.0 (n = 63)	621.0*** (n = 60)	960.0 (n = 130)	140.0*** (n = 121)
1986 Grievance Cases	95.3	50.4***	36.3	10.6***
1986 Interest Cases (mean)	4.2	4.2	3.4	2.9
Income from Arbitration			37.6%	17.3%***
Days per Month in Arbitration			7.3	3.4***

*** $p \leq .001$

criterion of ten years' experience in arbitration was selected as the cutoff point. The mainline arbitrators then became those arbitrators within this subgroup who had heard more than the median number of cases over their careers. For full-time arbitrators this meant a minimum of 1,200 career cases and for part-time practitioners it was 400 cases. The non-mainline cohort group consisted of those arbitrators who had more than ten years of experience but had heard less than the medians listed above. Under these criteria, full-time mainline arbitrators had heard more than three times as many cases over their career as their non-mainline colleagues and almost twice as many in 1986. The ratios for mainline and non-mainline part-time arbitrators were seven to one for career cases, almost four to one for 1986 cases, and two to one for the percentage of income from arbitration, and days per month spent in arbitration.

The mainline arbitrators were almost entirely white, non-hispanic men. Averaging 62 years in age and 24 years of experience, they did not differ materially from their non-mainline cohort group. They differed from the non-mainline group, however, in having more education: 63 percent of the full-time group were attorneys, and 46 percent of the part-timers were Ph.D.'s (as opposed to 55 and 38 percent for the other group). They also seemed to be much more focused on their profession. They were more active in professional labor relations organizations (AAA, FMCS, SPIDR, and FLRP) and a greater proportion of these arbitrators restricted their membership in professional societies to those that were tied into labor relations. Even though they were more heavily scheduled, almost half of the mainline group indicated a desire for more cases, as opposed to roughly one-third for their less busy counterparts.

Table 2.5
Sources of Cases for Mainline (ML) and Non-Mainline (NML) Arbitrators (1986)

	Full-Time		Part-Time	
	ML	NML	ML	NML
Source	Mean Number of Cases			
AAA	17.5	11.6 (X)	7.6	3.1 (X)
FMCS	16.5	12.1 (X)	10.5	5.5 (X)
State Agency	6.9	9.5 (X)	5.4	2.9 (X)
Permanent Panel	24.0	14.8 (*)	14.5	7.6 (*)
Permanent Umpire	16.9	10.2 (*)	12.1	2.1 (**)
Direct	20.0	15.5 (X)	7.3	4.0 (X)
Non-Union	4.9	4.4	1.9	3.1 (X)
	Percentages			
Public Sector	26.2	38.3***	29.3	42.4***
Private Sector	73.8	61.7***	70.7	57.8***

*p ≤ .05
**p ≤ .01
***p ≤ .001
(X)p ≤ .01 in weighted population but ns in unweighted survey group.

Not only did the mainline arbitrators decide more cases, but they secured their cases from a larger variety of sources (see Table 2.5). They received the larger number of cases from almost all of the principal sources of cases for arbitrators, with the differences being particularly striking in the number of cases received from permanent panels and permanent umpireships. In addition, almost three-quarters of the cases heard by the mainline arbitrators came from the private sector, a significantly higher proportion than for the non-mainline cohort group.

The Public Sector Arbitrator

One of the most important developments in labor relations since the 1960s has been the spread of unionization and collective bargaining to the public sector. A generation ago, public employee unions were largely restricted to the U.S. Postal Service, some school teachers and craft workers, and the employees of a few large Northeastern cities. Today more than five million government employees are covered by collective bargaining agreements. The percentage of public employees unionized more than doubles the percentage of private sector employees. The ar-

Table 2.6
Public Sector Activity (1986)

	Percentage of Caseload in the Public Sector	
	0-40 percent	41-100 percent
Number in Sample	322	180
Percent NAA***	74.2%	46.7%
Number in Population	1,309	1,196
Percent NAA***	30.2%	11.6%
	Mean Values	
Age***	59 years	54 years
Years of Experience***	21 years	18 years
Percent Women***	45.3%	54.7%
1986 Grievance Cases*	28.6	19.3
Percent of Pay from Arbitration (Part time only)**	26.0%	17.5%
Days per Month in Arbitration (Part time only)*	4.4	3.6
Cases in Career	476	192

*p ≤ .05
**p ≤ .01
***p ≤ .001
(X)p ≤ .01 in weighted population but ns in unweighted survey group.

bitration of grievances is almost as common in the public as it is in the private sector, and more than thirty states have passed interest arbitration laws.[16]

These changes are reflected in the practice of arbitration. Table 2.6 provides a "median split" of arbitrators on the basis of percentage of their caseload in the public sector. The dividing point between the two classes is 40 percent, meaning that roughly half of the arbitrators in the United States who heard at least one case in 1986 draw 40 percent or more of their cases from the public sector and the rest, less than 40 percent.

There were substantial differences between these arbitrators. Those who were most active in the public sector were, on average, five years younger and had three years less experience. They were much less likely to belong to the NAA and the bulk of the female arbitrators fell into this group.

Statistically significant differences also existed between the groups in terms of 1986 cases and career cases. Arbitrators who had *fewer* public sector cases decided *more* cases currently and had decided a much larger number of cases during their careers. The part-time arbitrators who had *fewer* public sector cases also earned a larger proportion of their income from arbitration.

The Ambitious Arbitrator

In the context of this chapter, there are two kinds of "ambitious" arbitrators. One kind consists of active part-time arbitrators who stated a desire to practice arbitration on a full-time basis and the second includes all the active arbitrators who said that they wanted to expand their practices. As Table 2.3f previously indicated, about 40 percent of the active part-time arbitrators in 1986 wanted to become full time, and half of the arbitration population desired more cases.

Several background variables were significantly related to both aspects of arbitral ambition. These variables were tied in to age, gender, experience, NAA membership, and cases. It was the younger, less experienced respondents, and often the women and the non-NAA members who expressed the strongest desire to expand their practice or move from a part-time to a full-time status. These are the arbitrators who typically have smaller practices currently and lower career caseloads. The older, more experienced arbitrators, whether full or part-time, seemed to be more content with their level of activity.

Some of the strongest relationships in the survey were the highly significant *negative* relationships between the desire for expansion of practice with age and experience. For example, less than 20 percent of the long-term part-time arbitrators wanted full-time practices, but almost half of the less experienced part-timers wanted to arbitrate full-time.

Women and Minorities

Only 32 women participated in the study, and all but ten of the respondents were non-whites or hispanics, a matter which will be discussed further in Chapter 6. Although the sample sizes were very small, they do not appear to differ greatly from the proportion of women and non-whites in the arbitral population. Because the sample sizes are so small, however, the generalizations are offered as "best judgment" rather than "proven fact."

The data suggest that minority group arbitrators resemble the rest of the population in being elderly, experienced, and well educated. The typical minority respondent was a 58-year-old man with sixteen years of arbitration experience. One of the ten minority respondents was a full-time arbitrator, three belonged to the NAA, two were women, six were attorneys, three had their Ph.D., and they were about as active in professional associations as the rest of the sample.

They resembled the other respondents in drawing about two-thirds of their cases from the private sector. But their practices were much smaller. At the median, they had heard twelve cases in the year prior to the survey (none more than fifty) and slightly over fifty in their career (none more than 500).

The women differed in a statistically significant way from the men in being, on average, about a decade younger and in having only one-third of the experience. The typical female arbitrator was 48 years old and had six years' experience (75% of the sample had less than ten years in arbitration). They were significantly more active than men in professional associations, particularly SPIDR, the FLRP, and the legal organizations, but a significantly smaller proportion were in the Academy.[17]

Although the difference was not statistically significant, the mean number of decisions rendered by female arbitrators in 1986 was higher than the number decided by men (roughly 30 as opposed to 23). But, reflecting their comparative youth and shorter careers, the total number of cases decided by the women in their career was far less than the number decided by the men. The mean career caseload for the men was 358 cases and the median was 196, while the mean for women was 120 and the median was 70. Only three of the female respondents had heard more than 1,000 cases in their career, while 108 men (more than 20% of the sample) had done so.

The structure of their caseloads was also quite different. Women get more cases from the public sector.[18] At the median, the female arbitrator secured roughly half of her cases from the public sector, while only 30 percent of the male arbitrators' cases came from government. Finally, almost every measure that dealt with the future indicated that the women wanted to expand their practices to a greater degree than the men: they wanted more cases now, more cases in the future, and more who were working part-time wanted full-time arbitration.

The Uncalled Arbitrator

All of the data discussed up to this point were based upon the responses of arbitrators who decided at least one case in 1986. With this section, the focus shifts to those arbitrators who said that they wanted cases but did not get any that year. As has been noted elsewhere in this book, more than 20 percent of the people listed as arbitrators received no cases in 1986. Many of these, however, said that they did not want cases. They indicated that they had removed themselves from the active ranks of arbitrators as a result of illness, retirement, loss of interest, or other responsibilities. But about 9 percent stated that they wanted cases but didn't get any in 1986. These arbitrators are discussed in this section.[19]

They resembled the rest of the sample in being elderly (a mean age of 57) and in being almost always white, non-hispanic men. They varied greatly in terms of experience. Eighteen percent had never had a case; 36 percent had heard their first case between one and ten years in the past; and the remainder had between eleven and 41 years of arbitration experience. None of these arbitrators had large practices: they had heard a mean of seven cases; none had heard over 100 cases; and none had been elected to the National Academy. They differed from the active arbitrators largely in these areas:

(1) The primary offices of 40 percent were in three states: Pennsylvania (20%), New York, and Florida (9% apiece).

(2) They came from the legal rather than the academic wing of the profession. Almost 60 percent were attorneys and only 17 percent had a Ph.D.

(3) They were much less involved in professional associations. Active arbitrators joined industrial relations and labor law associations at double or triple the rates of the uncalled arbitrators. For example, the two most popular associations among arbitrators are the AAA and the IRRA. More than 70 percent of the active arbitrators in the study belonged to those associations, but less than 40 percent of the uncalled arbitrators belonged to the AAA and 26 percent to the IRRA.

Briggs and Anderson called attention to the relationship between "visibility characteristics" and caseload. The arbitrators who were busy kept themselves visible through such activities as professional associations where, among other things, they can meet clients. Perhaps one of the keys to the non-existent caseload of these arbitrators is tied into their lower levels of participation in the societies related to their field.

Summary and Conclusions

The NAA study shows that arbitrators have not changed very much over the years in many basic characteristics. In 1986 they were still, for the most part, elderly, white, non-hispanic males. They were well educated, although they came from a variety of scholastic backgrounds. Most of them had graduate training: almost one-third had doctorates; and over half were attorneys.

Arbitration usually represents a second career. Typically the arbitrator comes from teaching or the practice of law. A substantial number have also come from human resource management, but few have entered from the labor movement.

Arbitrators are active in many organizations associated with labor relations or labor law but they tend to refrain from joining other organizations. This tendency to focus on career-related societies is most strong among busy, full-time arbitrators. Although many are contented with their careers, a substantial number want to increase their caseload, and these are usually the younger arbitrators, generally those who practice on a part-time basis, often the women, and almost always, those with a comparatively small practice.

In 1986, four out of five active arbitrators worked at their profession part-time. Typical part-timers hear about fifteen cases a year, work about four days a month at arbitration, and make close to one-fifth of their income from it. Full-time arbitrators, on the average, hear approximately 65 cases a year. Up to 1986, the typical active part-time arbitrator had heard almost 200 cases and the full-time practitioner, close to 900 cases. Not surprisingly, the highly experienced arbitrators had the largest caseloads and were the most likely members of the NAA. Interestingly, while there is a strong relationship between caseload and experience, there is no relationship between activity in interest arbitration and experience.

Women remain a minority group within the field. The typical female arbitrator is younger and less experienced than the male and more active in the public sector. Her current caseload compares with that of the man but her career caseload is far smaller. The women indicated a stronger desire than the men for more cases or for a change from part-time to full-time status.

The younger, less experienced arbitrators and the women tend to be more active in the public sector than their older, more experienced colleagues. It is likely that the growth of bargaining in the public sector provided them a passageway into the field. These arbitrators also indicate the strongest desire to increase their activity. These considerations fit harmoniously because, strangely enough, a high level of activity in the public sector is related to a lighter overall caseload and a desire to increase it.

The chief difference between the arbitrators who are not called for cases and the rest of the profession seems to be related to membership in professional associations (they are far less active in these organizations which often provide *entrée* to clients) and perhaps to location (Pennsylvania is particularly ridden with uncalled arbitrators).

Notes

We are grateful to Walter and Gladys Gershenfeld, fellow NAA members, and Robert Schindler, of the Rutgers Camden School of Business, for their critical reading and their comments. The authors also wish to acknowledge the assistance given them by Madhukar B. Golhar of the Bureau of Government Research, Rutgers University, and Walter Tymon, then Assistant Professor of Management at the Rutgers Camden Business School, for their help with the computer analysis. We also thank Joanne Santry from the secretarial staff of the Rutgers Camden School of Business for typing the tables.

1. Except for the one section that deals with arbitrators who received no cases, all of the analysis in this chapter is based upon the responses of 529 arbitrators who decided at least one case in 1986. The analysis uses the standard statistical tests—chi square and "t" tests on the entire sample and on selected subgroups within the sample. The expansion weights described in Chapter 1 have been used throughout the chapter although the tables also indicate the actual number of respondents.

2. Edgar L. Warren and Irving Bernstein, "A Profile of Labor Arbitration," *Industrial and Labor Relations Review* 4, no. 2 (1951), pp. 200–222. Over two years, 238 arbitrator respondents reported that they had heard 878 contract cases and 7,623 grievances. Their average per diem was $89 on contract cases and $75 on grievances.

3. Robert Coulson, "Spring Checkup on Labor Arbitration Procedure," *Labor Law Journal* 16, no. 5 (1965), pp. 259–265.

4. James F. Power, "Improving Arbitration: Roles of Parties and Agencies," *Monthly Labor Review* 95, no. 11 (1972), pp. 15–22.

5. Donald J. Petersen and Julius Rezler, "Fee Setting and Other Administrative Practices of Labor Arbitrators," *Labor Arbitration Reports* 68 (1977), pp. 1383–1396.

6. Steven S. Briggs and John C. Anderson, "An Empirical Investigation of Arbitrator Acceptability," *Industrial Relations* 19, no. 2 (1980), pp. 163–174.

7. Perry A. Zirkel, "A Profile of Grievance Arbitration Cases," *Arbitration Journal* 38, no. 1 (1983), pp. 35–38. Data on the public/private sector breakdown are available in AAA's newsletter, *Study Time* (July 1982, October 1984, January 1986, January 1987, January 1988, and December 1989).

8. Brian L. King, "Some Aspects of the Active Labor Arbitrator," *Personnel Journal* 50, no. 2 (1971), pp. 115–123.

9. Herbert G. Heneman III and Marcus H. Sandver, "Arbitrators' Backgrounds and Behaviors," *Journal of Labor Research* 4, no. 2 (1983), pp. 115–124.

10. John Smith Herrick, "Profile of a Labor Arbitrator," *Arbitration Journal* 37, no. 2 (1982), pp. 18–21; and "Labor Arbitration As Viewed by Labor Arbitrators," *Arbitration Journal* 38, no. 1 (1983), pp. 65–67.

11. J. Timothy Sprehe and Jeffrey Small, "Members and Nonmembers of the National Academy of Arbitrators: Do They Differ?" *Arbitration Journal* 39, no. 3 (1984), pp. 25–33.

12. A. Dale Allen, Jr. and Daniel F. Jennings, "Sounding Out the Nation's Arbitrators: An NAA Survey," *Labor Law Journal* 39, no. 7 (1988), pp. 423–431. See also Jennings and Allen, "Labor Arbitration Costs and Case Loads: A Longitudinal Analysis," *Labor Law Journal* 41, no. 2 (1990), pp. 80–88.

13. The NAA studies have been reported in the *Proceedings of the Annual Meetings of the National Academy of Arbitrators* (Washington: BNA Books, Inc., 1957, 1959, 1964, 1965, 1971, 1974, and 1985).

14. Of all of these studies, Briggs and Anderson performed the most thorough analysis of the relationship between the arbitrator's background and career. They found that a few background characteristics (age, sex, law degree, apprenticeship, years of experience, and previous work experience) were positively related to the arbitrator's current caseload; that years of college and possession of a Ph.D. were negatively related to caseload; and that the completion of a formal arbitrator training program had a positive relationship to caseload. But none of these relationships remained statistically significant in multiple regression analysis.

15. Charles J. Coleman, *Managing Labor Relations in the Public Sector* (San Francisco: Jossey-Bass, Inc., 1990), pp. 223–225.

16. Ibid., Chapters 8 and 12.

17. Twelve of the 32 women (37.5%) in the sample were NAA members as opposed to almost two-thirds of the male respondents.

18. In one of the editorial conferences on this book, Marcia Greenbaum gave some hint as to why this might be so. She stated that she began to arbitrate about the time that public sector labor relations began to be important and most of her early cases were in the public sector. She thought that public sector selectors were much more receptive to female arbitrators because women played such a predominant role on so many government jobs. From a public sector base, she gained the experience and the acceptability to build a practice in the private sector.

19. Ninety-one respondents, representing more than 20 percent of the arbitrator population, reported no cases for 1986. Fifty-two indicated no desire for cases: they had retired entirely, had been ill or injured, or had left arbitration for something else. The remaining thirty-nine, representing 9 percent of the population, stated that they wanted cases but received none. These respondents are the subject of analysis in this section of the chapter.

3

Members of the National Academy of Arbitrators: Are They Different from Non-Academy Arbitrators?

William H. Holley, Jr.

The preceding chapter raised questions about the descriptive characteristics of the people who practice arbitration. This chapter follows up by examining the characteristics of those arbitrators elected to the National Academy. Are they different? If they are, how do they differ? Academy members have been referred to as "mainline" arbitrators, as distinguished from the "fringe" arbitrators who are trying to enter the mainstream.[1] Some labor agreements limit arbitrator selection to active Academy members, and a great number of labor and management advocates seek out Academy members when selecting arbitrators.[2]

To become a member of the National Academy of Arbitrators, applicants must meet the following membership standards:

(1) The applicant should be of good moral character, as demonstrated by adherence to sound ethical standards in professional activities. (2) The applicant should have substantial and current experience as an impartial arbitrator of labor-management disputes, so as to reflect general acceptability by the parties. (3) As an alternative to (2), the applicant with limited, but current experience in arbitration should have attained general recognition through scholarly publication or other activities as an impartial authority on labor-management relations.

Membership will not be conferred upon applicants who serve partisan interests as advocates or consultants for Labor or Management in labor-management relations or who are associated with or are members of a firm which performs such advocate or consultant work. (National Academy of Arbitrators, The Constitution and By-Laws, May 30, 1990)

The threshold standard for meeting the test of "substantial and current experience as an impartial arbitrator . . . to reflect general acceptability by the parties . . . '' has generally been applied to mean five years of arbitration experience with a minimum of fifty awards.[3] This chapter will show whether Academy members differ from the non-Academy arbitrators in terms of their demographics, memberships in organizations, employment, panel participation, sources of cases, caseloads and types of cases, fees and billing practices, additional offices, training interests, and participation in nontraditional areas of dispute resolution.

Demographic Characteristics

While the typical labor arbitrator is more likely to be older, male, white, married, and highly educated, do Academy members differ from non-Academy arbitrators in these demographic characteristics? Table 3.1 shows demographic differences between Academy members and non-Academy arbitrators who decided at least one case in 1986. The characteristics examined are age, gender, marital status, race, and educational background.

Age

The typical active Academy member was almost 60 years old in 1986, about five years older than the non-Academy arbitrator. This difference was expected given that the threshold requirement for Academy membership is fifty cases in five years. Likewise, the average age of the male and female Academy members exceeds the average age of their non-Academy counterparts, but only the difference in the average age of the male arbitrators is significant. The average ages of the male Academy members and non-Academy arbitrators are 59.9 and 56.3; the average ages of the female arbitrators are 55.4 and 46.4, respectively.

The average age of Academy members has gradually increased from the first survey of Academy membership in 1952. That year, the average age was just under 50; by 1962 it was 53 years of age. In 1987, there were 45 Academy members under 40 years old and 95 above the age of 65 with an age range from 33 to 83.

Gender

An overwhelming majority of active professional arbitrators in the 1987 sample are male: 96.4 percent (324 of 336) of the Academy members and 89.6 percent (173 of 193) of the non-Academy arbitrators. But these ratios are accurate reflections of the same ratios of male and female arbitrators

Table 3.1
Demographic Characteristics of Arbitrators: Non-NAA vs. NAA Arbitrators (1987)

Characteristics	Non-NAA Arbitrators	NAA Arbitrators
Average Age		
Total*	55.3 (n = 193)	59.8 (n = 336)
Males*	56.3 (n = 173)	59.9 (n = 324)
Females	46.4 (n = 20)	55.4 (n = 12)
	Percentages	
Gender**		
Male	89.6 (n = 173)	96.4 (n = 324)
Female	10.4 (n = 20)	3.6 (n = 12)
Martial Status		
Married	84.9 (n = 163)	91.6 (n = 306)
Divorced/Separated	9.9 (n = 19)	5.7 (n = 19)
Widowed	2.6 (n = 5)	2.1 (n = 7)
Never Married	2.6 (n = 5)	0.5 (n = 2)
Race		
White, non-hispanic	97.4 (n = 185)	99.4 (n = 331)
White, hispanic	0.5 (n = 1)	0
Black, non-hispanic	1.5 (n = 3)	0.3 (n = 1)
Black, hispanic	0	0
Asian	1.0 (n = 2)	0.3 (n = 1)
American Indian	0	0

*** p ≤ .001
** p ≤ .01
* p ≤ .05

in the population. Only 32 professional arbitrators in the sample are women; however, the percentage of non-Academy female arbitrators is significantly higher than the percentage of NAA female arbitrators. Women have only recently begun to enter the arbitrator profession in measurable numbers. One positive sign of increasing entry on the part of women is their recent influx into the Academy. A growing number of women arbitrators have met the membership requirements for entry into the Academy. For example, from 1988 to 1990, the National Academy of Arbitrators admitted fifty members; 16 percent were women. Mario Bognanno shows in Chapter 6 that after entry, the typical woman arbitrator does as well as the typical male in terms of cases heard. This suggests that *entry*, not *acceptability* is at issue.

Race

Without question, the profession of labor arbitration remains primarily a "white" profession. There is no statistically significant difference between the composition of the Academy and the non-Academy active arbitrators: 99.4 percent (331 of 333) of the Academy members and 97.4 percent (185 of 191) of the non-Academy arbitrators who completed the questionnaire are white. Although several development programs have been implemented to increase the number of minority arbitrators, there has been little progress. Of the 522 practicing arbitrators in the sample, only 1.5 percent are members of a minority group. The industrial relations community remains challenged to recruit minority entrants into the arbitration profession.

Marital Status

Although nearly 90 percent of the 1987 sample was married, the percentage of married Academy members was only slightly higher. The percentages of the practicing non-Academy arbitrators who were divorced/separated, widowed, or never married was only slightly higher than those of the Academy members. None of these differences were statistically significant.

Education

Among the arbitrators hearing at least one case in 1986, nearly all have at least an undergraduate degree and most have a law degree, a master's degree, or an earned doctorate (see Table 3.2). The majority of the arbitrators (56.3% of the non-Academy arbitrators and 58.6% of the Academy members) hold law degrees, but these percentages are not significantly different. Of the Academy members who did not have law

Table 3.2
Education Levels Attained by Non-NAA and NAA Arbitrators (1987)

Education	Non-NAA Arbitrators	NAA Arbitrators
	Percentages	
Law Degrees	56.3 (n = 108)	58.6 (n = 196)
In Addition to Law Degree, Highest Education Attained		
Master's	14.8 (n = 16)	25.6 (n = 50)
Doctorate	8.3 (n = 9)	6.7 (n = 13)

Of Those Not Having
  Law Degree, Highest
  Education Attained
	Total = 84	Total = 138

High School	4.0 (n = 3)	0 (n = 0)
Vocational/Technical	0 (n = 0)	0 (n = 0)
Two Year Associate	1.4 (n = 1)	1.5 (n = 2)
Bachelor's	9.5 (n = 7)	5.3 (n = 7)
Graduate Work	4.1 (n = 3)	1.5 (n = 2)
Master's	29.8 (n = 25)	24.6 (n = 34)
Doctorate	41.6 (n = 35)	63.8 (n = 88)

degrees, 63.8 percent had a doctorate, whereas of the 84 non-Academy arbitrators who did not have law degrees, 41.6 percent (35 of 84) had a doctorate. In addition, 6.7 percent of the Academy members and 8.3 percent of the non-Academy arbitrators who held law degrees also had doctorates.

About one-fourth of each group indicated that the master's degree was the highest degree earned: 24.6 percent for the Academy members and 29.8 percent for the non-Academy arbitrators. About one-fourth of Academy arbitrators and 15 percent of the 108 non-Academy arbitrators with law degrees also had a master's degree.

Organizational Memberships

Several professional organizations attract labor arbitrators as members. These organizations include the American Arbitration Association (AAA), the Industrial Relations Research Association (IRRA), the Society of Professionals in Dispute Resolution (SPIDR), the Society of Federal Labor Relations Professionals (FLRP), the Labor Law Section of regional bar associations, and the Labor Law Section of the American Bar Association (ABA). Academy members are more likely to belong to each of these organizations, that is, with the exception of the regional bar associations where non-Academy arbitrators had a higher membership percentage.

The AAA, a private professional organization that fosters arbitration as a dispute-resolution process, is the most popular for both groups. Table 3.3 shows that 84.7 percent of the Academy members and 65.4 percent of the non-Academy arbitrators were members of the AAA in 1987. Also, a significantly larger percentage of the Academy members were members of the IRRA (74.9% vs. 54.6%). The IRRA comprises educators, professional union and management officials, government officials, neutrals, and others interested in industrial relations research.

SPIDR brings together neutrals in various types of mediation, for example, divorce or community, and arbitration. SPIDR has attracted just over half of the Academy members, which is significantly more than the 41.3 percent of the non-Academy arbitrators. FLRP is composed of union and management officials as well as neutrals interested in labor relations (including arbitration) in the federal sector. Only a few active professional arbitrators were members of this organization; however, a significantly higher proportion of Academy (11.4%) than non-Academy arbitrators (3.2%) were members.

The ABA and the regional bar associations attract professional arbitrators having law degrees. Even though there was no difference in the percentage of Academy and non-Academy arbitrators having law degrees, significantly more Academy members (28.7%) than non-Academy arbi-

Table 3.3
Organizational Memberships of Non-NAA and NAA Arbitrators (1987)

Organizations	Non-NAA Arbitrators	NAA Arbitrators
	Percentages	
AAA***	65.4 (n = 123)	84.7 (n = 284)
IRRA***	54.6 (n = 103)	74.9 (n = 251)
SPIDR*	41.3 (n = 78)	51.3 (n = 172)
FLRP*	3.2 (n = 6)	11.4 (n = 38)
Labor Law Section/ Regional Bar	35.6 (n = 67)	36.4 (n = 122)
ABA**	18.1 (n = 34)	28.7 (n = 96)

*** $p \leq .001$
** $p \leq .01$
* $p \leq .05$

trators (18.1%) were members of the ABA Labor Law Section. More of each group belonged to their regional bar associations (36.4% of Academy arbitrators; 35.6% of non-Academy arbitrators), but there was no significant difference in the percentages of memberships between the two groups.

Employment Status of Arbitrators

Arbitration is a part-time profession for the majority of practicing arbitrators; however, there were significant differences between the employment status of Academy members and non-Academy arbitrators. Table 3.4 shows that 43.5 percent of the Academy members practiced arbitration on a full-time basis in 1986, but only 15 percent of the non-Academy arbitrators did.

These differences in arbitration practices are consistent with the differences in average percentage of gross income derived from work as a

Table 3.4
Employment Status of Non-NAA and NAA Arbitrators (1986)

Status	Non-NAA Arbitrators	NAA Arbitrators
	Percentages	
Full-time***	15.0 (n = 29)	43.5 (n = 146)
Part-time***	85.0 (n = 164)	65.5 (n = 190)
Part-time Only		
Gross Income Derived from Work as a Neutral**	17.9 (n = 160)	42.9 (n = 186)
Mean Full-time Equivalent Days/Month Worked As A Neutral***	3.32 (n = 152)	8.42 (n = 179)
Desire to Work Full-time As A Neutral**	41.6 (n = 161)	25.8 (n = 182)

*** $p \leq .001$
** $p \leq .01$
* $p \leq .05$

neutral. Academy members earned an average of 43 percent of their gross income from their arbitration practice, whereas non-Academy arbitrators earned only 18 percent. A major reason for the differences in earnings between the groups was the number of days worked per year. Academy members averaged just over eight days per month, a significantly higher average than the three days worked by the non-Academy arbitrators.

The differences in employment status among the arbitrators surveyed could change if the opportunity arises because significantly more of the non-Academy arbitrators (42%) than the Academy members (26%) wanted to work as arbitrators on a full-time basis. The majority of the Academy members who practice part-time and did not want to practice full-time listed "teacher" as their principal occupation before becoming an arbitrator. Further analysis shows that about three-fourths of Academy and one-half of non-Academy arbitrators who were teachers when they began arbitrating still preferred to practice only on a part-time basis. Just over 50 percent of the Academy and non-Academy arbitrators who were law-

Table 3.5
Principal Occupation of Part-time Non-NAA and NAA Arbitrators (1987)

Occupation	Non-NAA Arbitrators	NAA Arbitrators
	Percentages	
Administrator, Regulatory Body	1.2 (n = 2)	1.6 (n = 3)
Administrator, IR/HR	1.2 (n = 2)	2.1 (n = 4)
Consultant	4.9 (n = 8)	1.6 (n = 3)
Lawyer	32.7 (n = 53)	18.5 (n = 35)
Other Neutral-Mediator, Fact-finder	6.2 (n = 10)	2.1 (n = 4)
Teacher***	30.2 (n = 49)	54.5 (n = 103)

*** p ≤ .001
** p ≤ .01
* p ≤ .05

yers when they began arbitrating still practiced arbitration only on a part-time basis. Apparently those who arbitrated on a part-time basis have chosen to continue to do so. Table 3.5 shows the principal occupation of the arbitrators with part-time practices.

Arbitration Panels: Participation and Sources of Cases

Parties to arbitration select their presiding arbitrator from names provided by various agencies and organizations. A comparison of participation on arbitration panels shown in Table 3.6 reveals a significantly higher 1986 participation rate for active Academy members.

Both groups were most often listed on AAA panels; however, the Academy members' participation rate (94.9%) is significantly higher than the non-Academy arbitrators (74.9%). The next highest participation rate among all arbitrators was their presence on the FMCS roster of arbitrators.

Table 3.6
Participation on Arbitration Panels of Non-NAA and NAA Arbitrators (1986)

Arbitrator Panels	Non-NAA Arbitrators	NAA Arbitrators
	Percentages	
AAA***	74.9 (n = 143)	94.9 (n = 315)
FMCS***	61.7 (n = 118)	93.0 (n = 309)
State	58.6 (n = 112)	65.0 (n = 216)
Ad Hoc	11.5 (n = 22)	18.4 (n = 61)
Employer/Union***	35.5 (n = 66)	73.4 (n = 243)
Postal Service***	7.5 (n = 14)	24.7 (n = 82)
Steel Industry*	4.3 (n = 8)	10.5 (n = 35)
Other Permanent Panels*	14.5 (n = 27)	22.6 (n = 75)
Permanent Umpireship***	12.8 (n = 24)	34.5 (n = 110)

*** p ≤ .001
** p ≤ .01
* p ≤ .05

Again, the rate is significantly higher for Academy arbitrators (93.0 vs. 61.7%). Since applicants must submit five written cases to the FMCS before they are considered for inclusion on its roster of arbitrators and the AAA has no minimum case requirement, the AAA panels have a thirteen percent higher participation rate by the non-Academy arbitrators.

Academy members participated more frequently than their non-Academy counterparts on specialized panels, such as the U.S. Postal Service and steel industry panels, other permanent panels, and permanent

Table 3.7
Sources of Cases: NAA Arbitrators vs. Non-NAA Arbitrators (1986)

Sources of Cases	A. Percent of NAA Arbitrators Receiving Cases from this Source (n = 327)	B. Percent of Non-NAA Arbitrators Receiving Cases from this Source (n = 188)	Ratio of A to B
FMCS***	73.4	51.6	1.4
AAA***	74.8	52.7	1.4
Direct Selection***	70.9	36.2	2.0
State Panels	37.9	34.6	1.1
Permanent Panels***	59.8	21.5	2.8
Permanent Umpireships***	19.3	6.4	3.0

*** $p \leq .001$
** $p \leq .01$
* $p \leq .05$

umpireships. For example, 24.7 percent of the Academy members and 7.5 percent of the non-Academy arbitrators participated on the postal panel; on the steel industry panel, 10.5 percent and 4.3 percent. Significantly more Academy members were arbitrators on employer/union panels (73.4% vs. 35.5%) and permanent umpires (34.5% vs. 12.8%).

Participation on arbitration panels is not the only differentiating feature between Academy members and non-Academy arbitrators; the source of their cases is another. Table 3.7 shows a comparison between the major sources of cases from the various panels for Academy members and non-Academy arbitrators. For each source of cases, a significantly higher percentage of Academy members were selected for cases than their non-Academy counterparts. For three of these sources, direct appointments, permanent panels, and permanent umpireships, the Academy members were at least twice as likely to receive arbitrator selection. For only one source, state panels, was there no significant difference between sources for arbitrator selection.

Caseload and Types of Cases

Caseload data in Table 3.8 show that Academy members have decided significantly more grievance and interest arbitration cases over their careers as well as in 1986. Academy members have decided a lifetime average of just over 1,300 cases, more than triple the number of non-Academy arbitrators. In 1986, Academy members decided an average of

Table 3.8
Caseloads of Non-NAA vs. NAA Arbitrators (1986)

	(mean number)	
Cases	Non-NAA Arbitrators	NAA Arbitrators
Cases in Career***	408.3 (n = 193)	1,310.2 (n = 336)
Cases Per Year***	17.2 (n = 193)	57.4 (n = 336)
Grievance Cases in 1986***	16.0 (n = 193)	55.7 (n = 336)
Interest Cases in 1986**	1.2 (n = 60)	1.8 (n = 140)
Cases Refused in 1986***	0.9 (n = 91)	3.8 (n = 189)
Additional Cases that could have been scheduled in 1986	12.6 (n = 79)	14.5 (n = 165)
Cases Preferred in 1986***	28.3 (n = 63)	55.8 (n = 118)
Cases Preferred in 1987***	29.0 (n = 63)	55.2 (n = 113)
Cases Preferred in 1990***	35.8 (n = 56)	55.3 (n = 100)

*** $p \leq .001$
** $p \leq .01$
* $p \leq .05$

almost 56 grievance cases, nearly four times the number for non-Academy arbitrators. Although only a few interest cases were decided by both groups of arbitrators, Academy members decided half again as many.

More Academy members refused cases than the non-Academy arbitrators. Academy members refused an average of nearly four cases in 1986, which is significantly more than a single case average refused by the non-Academy arbitrators. Yet, a strong minority of each group could have scheduled and decided additional cases. Although 165 Academy members

Table 3.9
Arbitration Practice of Non-NAA and NAA Arbitrators (1986)

Average Number of Cases/Year	Non-NAA Arbitrators	NAA Arbitrators
	(percentages)	
0-20***	79.1 (n = 144)	21.6 (n = 72)
21-40***	11.0 (n = 20)	28.7 (n = 96)
Over 40***	9.9 (n = 18)	49.7 (n = 166)

*** $p \leq .001$

could have scheduled and decided an average of 14.5 additional cases, and 79 non-Academy arbitrators could have scheduled and decided an average of 12.6 additional cases, no significant differences in percentages existed between the two groups. Using the expansion weights described in Chapter 1, over 15,000 additional cases could have been scheduled and decided if willing arbitrators had been given the opportunity by the selecting parties. Given the reported shortage of qualified labor arbitrators, one could easily contend that the parties are not fully utilizing those arbitrators who are already available.

The respondents were asked about their preferred caseloads for 1986, 1987, and 1990. While Academy members preferred a higher caseload than the non-Academy arbitrators, they preferred about the same caseload over those years, about 55 cases per year. Non-Academy arbitrators preferred to increase their caseloads, but only from an average of 28.3 cases in 1986 to 35.8 cases in 1990.

The respondents were asked to compare their caseloads with that of five years ago. About 40 percent of each group said their caseloads were about the same. When asked whether their caseloads were higher or lower, most of the non-Academy arbitrators indicated that their caseloads were higher, whereas just less than a majority of the Academy members' caseloads were higher. Thus, it appears that some of the non-Academy arbitrators were achieving greater acceptability as reflected by the increasing caseload.

When the career caseload totals were considered in relation to number of years of arbitration practice, some interesting results were observed. Table 3.9 shows there were significant differences in the average number

Table 3.10
Public and Private Sector Cases of Non-NAA vs. NAA Arbitrators (1986)

Cases	Non-NAA Arbitrators	NAA Arbitrators
	(percentages)	
Public Sector***	46.9 (n = 183)	30.8 (n = 331)
Private Sector***	53.1 (n = 183)	69.2 (n = 331)

*** $p \leq .001$
** $p \leq .01$
* $p \leq .05$

of cases decided over the years by Academy members and non-Academy arbitrators. Nearly 80 percent of the non-Academy arbitrators averaged less than 20 cases per year as compared to only 21.6 percent of the Academy members. Of the 144 non-Academy arbitrators who average less than 20 cases per year over their careers, just over 30 percent are educators. Interestingly, 56 percent of these arbitrators did not want to practice arbitration on a full-time basis. In comparison, just over one-fifth of the Academy members have decided an average of less than 20 cases per year over their careers as arbitrators. Half of these arbitrators indicated that their principal occupation was that of an educator, and 15 percent were attorneys. Over 60 percent of the Academy members who have decided an average of less than 20 cases stated that they prefer not to have a full-time arbitration practice. On the other hand, nearly half of the Academy members have decided an average of more than 40 cases per year over their careers, whereas less than 10 percent of the non-Academy arbitrators have averaged this amount. Of those Academy members who have decided an average of more than 40 cases per year, less than 10 percent listed their principal occupation as law and 17 percent listed their principal occupation as an educator.

Caseload preferences also reveal the personal interests and preferences of the arbitrators. Most who preferred a reduced caseload wanted to slow down, desired more vacation time, planned to retire, or were getting older. Those who preferred a higher caseload indicated they could handle more cases, anticipated having more time, or wanted to arbitrate full-time.

Designating cases as private or public sector helps to differentiate between the Academy members and the non-Academy arbitrators. Table 3.10 indicates that Academy members spent most of their time on private sector cases and non-Academy arbitrators spent more of their time on public sector cases than Academy members. More specifically, nearly 70

Table 3.11
Fees and Billings, Non-NAA vs. NAA Arbitrators (1986)

Average Billings	Non-NAA Arbitrators	NAA Arbitrators
Total (excluding Expenses)***	$ 1,072.40 (n = 182)	$ 1,238.80 (n = 305)
Hearing Days***	13.9 (n = 165)	44.6 (n = 226)
Cancelled/Postponed***	1.7 (n = 166)	11.3 (n = 231)
Study Days***	16.6 (n = 165)	70.6 (n = 226)
Travel Days***	1.4 (n = 165)	7.7 (n = 231)
Executive Sessions***	0.2 (n = 165)	1.0 (n = 229)

*** $p \leq .001$
** $p \leq .01$
* $p \leq .05$

percent of the cases decided by Academy members were in the private sector compared with only 53 percent of those decided by non-Academy arbitrators. This disparity is partially explained by the fact that about 59 percent of the non-Academy arbitrators participated on state arbitration panels responsible for deciding non-federal public sector cases. Although 58.3 percent of the non-Academy arbitrators were also listed on state arbitration panels, a lower proportion than for the Academy members, there was no significant difference in the percentages listed.

Fees and Billing Practices

Fees and billing days were significantly higher for the Academy members. Table 3.11 shows that the fees and billing days account for those arbitrators' higher earnings, which are presented and analyzed in Chapter 6. The Academy members' average billing for all cases was $1,238.80; the non-Academy arbitrators', $1,072.40. The total billing is composed primarily of the per diem, docketing, and cancellation fees. Table 3.12 shows the average per diem fee for grievance arbitration cases was $435.95

Table 3.12
Fees of Non-NAA vs. NAA Arbitrators (1986)

Average Fees	Non-NAA Arbitrators	NAA Arbitrators
	(means)	
Grievance Cases:		
Per Diem***	$ 374.89 (n = 188)	$ 435.95 (n = 330)
Docketing	$ 64.17 (n = 189)	$ 82.25 (n = 28)
Cancellation***	$ 180.86 (n = 187)	$ 347.74 (n = 322)
Interest Cases:		
Per Diem***	$ 365.00 (n = 58)	$ 472.61 (n = 136)
Docketing***	$ 47.50 (n = 2)	$ 68.75 (n = 8)
Cancellation***	$ 145.43 (n = 58)	$ 315.05 (n = 118)

*** p ≤ .001
** p ≤ .01
* p ≤ .05

for Academy members and $374.89 for non-Academy arbitrators. The average cancellation fee for Academy members was $347.74, but only $180.86 for non-Academy arbitrators. A docketing fee was charged by about five percent of the arbitrators, and the average docketing fee charged by these arbitrators was $69.00.

In interest arbitration cases, the average per diem fee charged by Academy members was $472.61, an amount that is significantly higher than the $365.00 charged by non-Academy arbitrators. Interestingly, Academy members charge about $37.00 more for interest cases than for grievance cases, whereas the non-Academy arbitrators charged about $10.00 less for interest arbitration cases. Likewise, the Academy members' cancellation fee for interest arbitration cases—$315.05—was significantly higher than the average fee charged by non-Academy arbitrators—$133.33. The

Table 3.13
Additional Offices of Non-NAA vs. NAA Arbitrators (1986)

	Non-NAA Arbitrators	NAA Arbitrators
Arbitrators Having Additional Offices (N.S.)	18.2% (n = 34)	22.5% (n = 72)

N.S. = Not Significant

docketing fee for interest arbitration cases was seldom charged; however, when it was charged, it averaged $56.00.

The average number of billing days was significantly greater for Academy members than non-Academy arbitrators, and the number of hearing days averaged 44.6 and 13.9 days, respectively. Academy members reported more postponed or cancelled hearings (11.31 vs. 1.7). They charged significantly more study days, 70.6, than their non-Academy counterparts, 16.6. Although travel days were proportionately lower, there was a significant difference between the number of travel days charged by Academy members and non-Academy arbitrators (7.7 vs. 1.4). Only a few days were charged for executive sessions, which were usually more closely associated with interest arbitration cases. Still, Academy members averaged significantly more billing days, 1.0, than the non-Academy arbitrators, 0.2. These data clearly show that the Academy members' fees as well as their billing days were significantly higher.

Additional Offices

Arbitrators establish more than one office for a number of reasons. One reason is to increase the geographical coverage of their practices (arbitrators are instructed by the appointing agencies to charge the parties for travel time and expenses from the nearest office of record). Another reason for additional offices is that some arbitrators migrate to second homes in the South or Southwest during cold weather. Table 3.13 shows about one arbitrator in five sets up a second office, but there is no significant difference between Academy members and non-Academy arbitrators. There is no difference in the number of full-time and part-time arbitrators who set up one or more additional offices. Also, there is no difference in the caseloads, per diem rates, and average bills for arbitrators who had only one office and those who had more than one.

Table 3.14
Types of Training Needed in Next Five Years˙ by Non-NAA and NAA Arbitrators (1987)

	Non-NAA Arbitrators[1]	NAA-Arbitrators[2]
Workshops, Refresher Courses, Simulation Seminars	15.2	27.5
Specific and In-depth Training in Complex Issues	19.3	17.5
Drugs and Drug Testing	11.0	7.5
NAA Education Conferences and Meetings	14.2	3.3

˙ Only the first two responses were counted.

[1] 56 did not respond; 17 indicated no need for training; 120 responded.

[2] 88 did not respond; 51 indicated no need for training; 197 responded.

Training Needs in the Next Five Years

The arbitrators in the study were asked to indicate the type of training that could benefit them over the next five years. While 40 percent of the arbitrators either did not respond or indicated no need for training and no statistically significant differences between groups were detected, there were some meaningful responses and slight differences between Academy members and non-Academy arbitrators.

Table 3.14 shows that the greatest need for training was for workshops, refresher courses, and simulation seminars, and there were more non-Academy arbitrators who expressed need for these types of training. This response is explained by the fact that the non-Academy arbitrators are generally the less experienced arbitrators. Both groups expressed a need for specific and in-depth training on complex issues, such as evidential rulings; however, there was only a slight difference in the percentage of responses. About 10 percent expressed a need for training in drug and drug testing cases; here also there was no difference between groups. Finally, 14.2 percent of the Academy members expressed need for NAA education conferences and meetings; only 3.3 percent of the non-Academy listed this need. This difference is explained by the fact that most non-Academy arbitrators have not attended NAA education conferences, which are held exclusively for members, or annual meetings to which guests are invited.

Dispute Resolution in Non-Traditional Areas

Nonunion Sector

Although the professional literature has recently focused on arbitration in the nonunion sector, few in either group of arbitrators have participated in this process. Table 3.15 suggests that about 25 percent of active Academy members and 15 percent of active non-Academy arbitrators have decided cases in the nonunion sector. These arbitrators averaged about four nonunion cases in 1986. Thus, arbitration in the nonunion sector remains low, but this arena is potentially useful for arbitration dispute resolution.

Dispute Resolution Other Than Arbitration

Less than half of the Academy members and non-Academy arbitrators participated in mediation, med-arb, or fact-finding. A greater percentage of the Academy members are active in the other forms of dispute resolution (48.0% vs. 36.1%); however, there was not much difference in the number of cases in which the two groups were involved. About one-fourth of the Academy and non-Academy arbitrators mediated one or more cases in 1986, but the average number of cases mediated by the non-Academy arbitrators was significantly higher (9.2 vs. 6.7).

Almost 20 percent of the Academy members and 13 percent of the non-Academy arbitrators participated in any med-arb cases during 1986. There was no significant difference in the average number of cases decided by the two groups (7.7 for non-Academy arbitrators; 7.6 for Academy members).

Roughly one-quarter of the arbitrators were active in the fact-finding process. The average number of cases was 3.5 for the Academy members and 3.7 for the non-Academy arbitrators, not a significant difference.

Alternative Dispute Resolution (ADR)

Neither Academy members nor non-Academy arbitrators were much involved in alternative dispute resolution. Less than 3 percent of the non-

Table 3.15
Participation in Forms of Dispute Resolution Other Than Traditional Arbitration by Non-NAA vs. NAA Arbitrators (1986)

Forms of Dispute Resolution	Non-NAA Arbitrators	NAA Arbitrators
Average Number of Cases in Nonunion Sector***	4.3 (n = 30)	3.5 (n = 85)
Arbitrators Involved in Other Dispute Resolution Procedures**	36.1% (n = 183)	48.0% (n = 323)
Average Number of Cases Mediated (N.S.)†	9.2* (n = 44)	6.7 (n = 96)
Average Number of Cases in Med-Arb*	7.7 (n = 26)	7.6 (n = 63)
Average Number of Cases Involving Factfinding (N.S.)	3.7 (n = 36)	3.5 (n = 94)
Average Number of Alternative Dispute Resolution (ADR) Cases (N.S.)	6.0 (n = 26)	6.0 (n = 42)
Arbitrators who expect greater share of cases in areas other than arbitration (N.S.)	29.5%	21.8%

*** $p \leq .001$
** $p \leq .01$
* $p \leq .05$
N.S. = Not Significant
† Average biased upward by one individual reporting 160 mediation cases.

Academy and Academy arbitrators were involved, with an average of 6 cases for both groups. No community/neighborhood, intercorporate, environment, family/divorce, or court-annexed disputes were resolved by ADR; the only ADR cases reported were commercial. Either labor arbitrators were not involved in ADR, or other types of arbitrators were performing the ADR service. Only 21.8 percent of the Academy members and 29.5 percent of the non-Academy arbitrators expected their non-labor arbitration caseloads to increase. Further, there is no significant difference in their predictions.

Conclusion

This study shows that Academy members and non-Academy arbitrators differ significantly in several demographic characteristics and their professional arbitration practices. As of 1987, Academy members were older, with more years of education. A greater proportion were married, male, and white, non-hispanic. They were more likely to be members of professional organizations that attract professional arbitrators, and a higher proportion participated on various arbitration panels and received case appointments via those panels. For 1986, a significantly higher percentage of Academy members were employed full-time as arbitrators, and they earned a higher percentage of their income from their arbitration practices than did their non-Academy counterparts. Likewise, they have decided more cases in their careers, as well as in 1986; charged higher fees, worked more days in arbitration, and charged more billing days for arbitration.

Significantly more of the cases decided by Academy members involve private sector parties. Although about one-fifth of the arbitrators had more than one office, multiple offices yielded no significant difference in the number of cases decided. Likewise, there was no significant difference between the number of Academy members and non-Academy arbitrators who had more than one office.

Both groups expressed interest in training and professional development. A greater proportion of non-Academy arbitrators expressed interest in workshops, refresher courses, and simulation exercises, whereas the Academy members preferred NAA educational institutes and meetings. Finally, only a few arbitrators in both groups decided any cases in areas other than labor arbitration, and only about one-fifth expected to increase the percentage of cases in these non-traditional areas.

These findings support the conclusion that professional arbitrators should aspire to be members of the Academy for self-interest, and for professional and personal reasons. They should have this aspiration for self-interest reasons, because the evidence supports the conclusion that Academy members have higher caseloads and consequently higher earnings. While Academy membership and caseload are positively correlated, the cause and effect are less clear. Since one needs to be on a proven success path as an arbitrator to gain admission to the Academy, it is not clear whether membership encourages professional success or vice versa. In addition, the annual Academy meeting in the spring of each year and the Academy's Continuing Education Conference in the fall of each year provide professional development and educational reasons for Academy membership. These meetings, plus the various regional meetings, create opportunity for professional growth, developing personal interactions, building camaraderie among professional arbitrators, and building close, personal relationships.

Notes

1. Paul Prasow and Edward Peters, *Arbitration and Collective Bargaining* (New York: McGraw Hill Book Company, 1983), p. 352.
2. Walter E. Baer, *The Labor Arbitration Guide* (Homewood, Illinois: Dow Jones-Irwin, Inc., 1974), p. 18; Walter E. Baer, *Winning in Labor Arbitration* (Chicago: Crain Books, 1982).
3. Ralph T. Seward, "Report of the Special Committee on Professionalism," in *Arbitration 1987: The Academy at Forty*, Proceedings of the 40th Annual Meeting of the National Academy of Arbitrators, ed. Gladys W. Gruenberg (Washington: BNA Books, Inc., 1988), p. 224.

Bibliography

"Report of the Committee on Research and Education: Survey of the Arbitration Profession in 1952," in *The Profession of Labor Arbitration*, ed. Jean T. McKelvey (Washington: BNA Books, Inc., 1957), pp. 176–182.
"Report of the Special Committee to Review Membership and Related Policy Questions of the Academy—Otherwise Known as the Reexamination Committee," in *Arbitration—1976*, eds. Barbara D. Dennis and Gerald G. Somers (Washington: BNA Books, Inc., 1976), pp. 361–386.
"Survey of Arbitration in 1962," in *Labor Arbitration: Perspectives and Problems*, ed. Mark Kahn (Washington: BNA Books, Inc., 1964), pp. 292–316.
"Survey of the Arbitration Profession in 1969," in *Arbitration and the Public Interest*, eds. Gerald Somers and Barbara D. Dennis (Washington: BNA Books, Inc., 1971), pp. 275–303.

4

Entry and Acceptability in the Arbitration Profession: A Long Way To Go

Joseph Krislov

According to Douglas Hall, a career is an ongoing sequence of events that represents an entire life in a work setting.[1] A career is built upon a series of choices that the individual makes in an attempt to realize some form of self-fulfillment from work and make a satisfactory living in the process. A career includes the education and training that prepares people for their work and the employment experiences that take place throughout their working lives.

This chapter examines the data from the NAA study from the perspective of the arbitral career, emphasizing entry into the profession and advancement within it. It attempts to create a career development model of our respondents, both members of the NAA and nonmembers. Using literature on careers as a basis, the arbitrator's career is divided into:

The Years of Preparation: The years that are spent in education and on jobs in related areas that trigger the individual's interest in the field.

Entry and Acceptability: The years when new arbitrators enter the profession and attempt to build practices.

The Journeyman Years: The years when arbitrators have widespread acceptance and recognition. For many arbitrators, this period includes years well beyond the normal retirement age in other occupations.

The preparation phase for all occupations typically includes a period of time devoted to education. For almost all arbitrators, it also includes the time they worked at other occupations before being selected to ar-

Table 4.1
Career Development (Medians)

	Year Born	Age When Received Highest Degree	Age When Decided First Case	Age When Elected to Academy	Cases in Career	Grievance Cases in 1986
All	1929 (n = 446)	31	47	49	120	25
NAA	1925 (n = 295)	29	42	49	700	40
Non-NAA	1930 (n = 151)	31	48	not applicable	65	6

The sample size for this table is slightly smaller than for other tables because it includes only respondents who answered all of the questions pertaining to age, year of highest degree, year of first case, NAA status, and cases in career. Failure to answer any of these questions led to elimination. Expansion weights have been applied to the data in all Chapter 4 tables: 11.0114 for non-NAA and 1.6536 for NAA responses.

bitrate. From our perspective, an individual's first award marks the end of the preparation period and the beginning of the second phase of the arbitral career.

For most arbitrators, this second period, entry and acceptability, is marked by an increasing caseload. For members of the Academy, this period is the time between the first award and their time of election to the NAA. For those arbitrators who are not Academy members, however, it is more difficult to delineate the boundaries between the preparation period and the third phase.

For many arbitrators this third period—the "journeyman years"—is a period of substantial reward. As is well known, admission to the Academy usually comes at an advanced age, and many arbitrators work well past the age of normal retirement. In examining the journeyman phase, the work patterns of older arbitrators are analyzed separately to determine how long they remain active and their level of activity.

As has been indicated, a particular event is assumed to mark the end of one phase and the beginning of another. Several key events in an individual's professional career have been determined for both members and nonmembers, and the median year and attained age for both groups are presented in Table 4.1. Specifically, the table indicates the arbitrator's year of birth, the year the arbitrator received a college degree, the year of the arbitrator's first award, and the year Academy members were admitted into the organization. In addition, the table includes data on an individual's career caseload as well as the grievance load in 1986.

Phase 1: The Years of Preparation

The Triggering Events

What stimulates a person's interest in an arbitration career? The respondents were asked to describe the "two main events/experiences"

Table 4.2
The Triggering Experiences

	Percentages
1. Advocacy	25.9 (n = 125)
2. Government Agency	15.0 (n = 79)
3. Educational	14.7 (n = 80)
4. Catch-all Response	10.0 (n = 49)
5. Experience in Labor Relations	6.8 (n = 26)
6. Apprenticeship or Intern	5.6 (n = 29)
7. Other	18.3 (n = 75)
8. Non-Respondents	3.7 (n = 26)

Expansion weights have been applied to the data.

that caused them to become arbitrators. The responses varied widely and they were grouped into eleven categories: (1) educational, (2) advocacy, (3) work with a government agency in labor relations, (4) work with a government agency outside of the field of labor relations, (5) service as a neutral, (6) friendship/relationship with an arbitrator, (7) teaching, (8) apprenticeship, (9) request to serve, (10) experience in labor relations, and (11) similar work in labor-related field or business. The diversity of responses indicates that many factors lead people into arbitration.

Most respondents thought in terms of a single event or experience. Over 40 percent failed to list a second main event/experience, and of those who did, 10 percent listed experiences outside the eleven defined categories. Consequently, it seemed unlikely that any insights would come from analyzing the second choice.

Table 4.2 lists the half dozen events or experiences that the largest number of respondents identified as triggering their interest in arbitration. These were selected by about three-quarters of the arbitrators. At the top of the list, with more than one-quarter of the responses, came advocacy in labor relations—as an attorney or as a management or union participant in contract negotiation or administration. The second experience was government service in labor relations—working for agencies such as the National War Labor Board, the National Labor Relations Board, or a state agency. Educational experiences came in third place—including formal education in labor relations and specialized training courses in topics such as mediation. About 15 percent of the arbitrators selected these two options. Ten percent of the arbitrators came into the field because of a catch-all response, which included being asked to serve, early retirement from another occupation, a desire to be self-employed, and passage of a state labor relations law. About 7 percent responded that some "experience in labor relations" triggered their interest.

Finally, almost 6 percent came into arbitration as a result of an internship program. A 1980 Academy report concluded "that the intern process . . . is the best way to train new arbitrators and gives them an opportunity to establish themselves."[2] In a sense, of course, they would not have been in the program unless there had been an earlier motivating interest. Nevertheless, the number of responses suggests that an internship program is a significant source of practicing arbitrators.

Education

Recruitment into a professional career typically begins in college. More specialized recruitment often takes place in graduate and professional schools, and some professional fields require additional years of study and/or a period of internship.

As is the case with other professionals, arbitrators are well educated. It is extremely rare to find an arbitrator without a college degree and a very large percentage have graduate degrees. As the previous two chapters have reported, almost 60 percent of U.S. arbitrators have degrees in law; over 20 percent possess a master's degree; and almost one-quarter hold doctorates. Whether the advanced degrees are "needed" for the practice of arbitration or whether "credentialism" aids acceptance, it is clear that arbitrators are well educated.

But unlike many other professions, there is no prescribed course of study that leads into arbitration. For many regulated professions, such as law and medicine, the training necessary to enter the field is prescribed, and completion of the entry requirements leads to licensure or certification. Not only do arbitrators differ in the level of education and the kind of degree, but they study different subjects. When the respondents were asked about the field in which they received their highest degree, four areas emerged as the "major disciplines": economics, IR/HR, liberal arts, and business. Two-thirds of the arbitrators in the study majored in one of these areas.

Pre-Arbitration Work Experience

The entry requirement for some occupations consists almost entirely of education: attorneys, accountants, or engineers secure their first position after completing law school or an undergraduate program. For other occupations a period of internship is required: physicians, for example, serve an internship or residency before beginning practice. Other occu-

Table 4.3
Positions Held by Arbitrators

A. The Principal Occupations Held by Arbitrators Immediately Prior to Entering Arbitration

	Percentages		
	All	NAA	Non-NAA***
Law	31.3 (n = 162)	30.1 (n = 101)	31.6 (n = 61)
Teaching	29.4 (n = 193)	42.6 (n = 143)	25.9 (n = 50)
Management (Industrial Relations/ Human Resources and Consultant)	17.6 (n = 76)	11.6 (n = 39)	19.2 (n = 37)
Neutral (Administration, Mediator, Fact-finder)	13.0 (n = 58)	9.2 (n = 31)	14.0 (n = 27)

B. Full-Time Position in IR/HR or Union Official

Union Official	9.9 (n = 48)	8.3 (n = 29)	10.4 (n = 20)
Industrial Relations/ Human Resources	32.6 (n = 155)	26.5 (n = 89)	34.3 (n = 66)

***$p \leq .001$, expansion weights have been applied to the data.

pations require a period of on-the-job training: the skilled trades, for example, normally ask for several years of apprenticeship before the entrant can become a fully qualified technician. Arbitrators almost always spend a number of years in another occupation before they enter the field.

The respondents were asked to identify the principal occupation they had held before they became labor arbitrators, and the results are listed in Table 4.3. These responses confirm the conventional view that very few individuals enter arbitration directly. Less than 2 percent of U.S. arbitrators reported being a student as their principal occupation before entering arbitration. Thus, virtually all of the arbitrators in the sample worked at some occupation before becoming arbitrators.

Because law and graduate study characterize the educational background of arbitrators, it is not surprising that law and teaching were the chief occupations that arbitrators held immediately before entering the profession. Roughly 60 percent of the arbitrators held jobs in law or teaching right before they became arbitrators. A third source, providing more than one-sixth of today's arbitrators, consisted of former management employees—either employees in the industrial relations/human resource function (IR/HR) or consultants. An additional 13 percent of the arbitrators came into the profession from positions as non-arbitrating neutrals (mediators and fact-finders) or administrators with governmental regulatory bodies.

Nine out of 10 of today's arbitrators came into arbitration from one of these four occupations. The two most important springboards into arbitration were teaching and the law, and two significant but less important launching pads were managerial work, most often in IR/HR, and government work as a neutral in labor relations.

There are differences in the occupational backgrounds of members of the Academy and nonmembers. The distributions for the four occupational groupings listed in Table 4.3 differ in a statistically significant way. Accounting for the statistical significance are the differences between members and nonmembers who reported teaching and management backgrounds. Over 40 percent of the NAA members came into arbitration from teaching, compared with 26 percent of nonmembers. On the other hand, almost one-fifth of the nonmembers had management backgrounds, almost double the percentage of NAA members.

Perhaps some of the success of teachers might be the fact that, coming from the academic world, they are perceived more readily as neutrals. This perception would enhance their acceptability. Arbitrators with management backgrounds might have a more difficult task achieving the "neutral" image and Academy membership.

Looking at the entire pre-arbitral work career, rather than simply at the job held immediately prior to entering arbitration, it is apparent that a large number of arbitrators have worked either for an organization in some IR/HR position or as a full-time union official. Almost one-third of the arbitrators worked in IR/HR and about 10 percent held a full-time union job before they entered arbitration (Table 4.3). These experiences provide good background because they expose an aspiring arbitrator to day-to-day labor problems, thus providing "hands-on" practical experience unlikely to be gained in formal education.

Is there a relationship between this aspect of an arbitrator's background and NAA status? The data, while not statistically significant, parallel the findings reported above. More nonmembers than members reported that they had held a full-time position in management or as a union representative. In addition, they worked in those positions longer. NAA members who had worked for a union, worked for about three years, and if they worked for management, an average of ten years. The corresponding figures for nonmembers were six years and thirteen years. Once again the data suggest that factors which help the parties identify the arbitrator with either management or union appear to impede the development of an arbitration career.

Phase 2: Entry and Gaining Acceptability

Models of career development usually suggest that entry into an individual's "stable work period" begins sometime between the ages of 20 and 35.[3] Assuming that the years of preparation come to an end when entrants into arbitration secure their first case, a typical arbitration career begins at a much later age. Because of the years spent in graduate work or the study of law, the typical arbitrator finishes formal education at about age 30 and then begins to work (Table 4.1).

But arbitrators need more than a good education to be selected for cases. Some work experience in a related field appears to be a necessary part of preparation—a period of time to make contacts, gain some seasoning, and perhaps lose some hair or have hair turn gray. From the parties' perspective, emphasis on age and experience may substitute for licensing or certification programs. Because arbitrators are neither licensed nor certified, the parties create their own form of protection against selecting an incompetent arbitrator by insisting upon age and experience.

NAA members rendered their first award at age 42, thirteen years after receiving their highest degrees. For nonmembers it was age 48, seventeen years after receiving their highest degrees. Members and nonmembers clearly enter the profession much later than individuals in other fields. But those who would later be elected to the NAA were able to achieve entry earlier than nonmembers (Table 4.1).

Building the Career

Most arbitrators and would-be arbitrators lament the long period of time waiting for the first few cases. Richard I. Bloch, a full-time, successful NAA arbitrator, undoubtedly reflected the views of many when he reported:

It has been my experience that one makes a very slow start in this profession, and should steel oneself for that in two ways, either by having another job on which to rely until one's caseload builds up, or by buying a lot of novels to read while waiting for the phone to ring. In my first year I had one case. During the second year my practice exploded: I had six cases.[4]

Not only do many arbitrators wait a long time for their first few cases, but it also takes time to build a practice. Most arbitration assignments are made on an ad-hoc basis and require both parties' approval. Acceptance in one collective bargaining relationship does not necessarily lead to acceptance in another. Thus, an aspiring arbitrator has to be acceptable to many parties—not simply one employer in the typical employment relationship. Moreover, arbitration ethics preclude some forms of solicitation. There are, of course, some activities (writing, teaching, presenting papers at meetings, and attending labor/management seminars) that serve to make one's availability known.[5] But even these more subtle "solicitation" efforts take time and often prove unsuccessful.

Arbitration is, therefore, a second career. It is an occupation that one enters after achieving recognition and status elsewhere. In some respects, arbitration resembles the physician engaged in a public health practice. A 1966 study of the careers of public health physicians and other medical specialists indicated that only 20 percent of those employed in public health "entered that specialty directly." In contrast, "over half to two-thirds" of other medical specialists began their working careers in their respective specializations. Further, about half of those working in public health worked in another field before entering public health. In contrast, only 3 percent of the surgeons and 8 percent of the internists worked in other specializations before entering these fields.[6]

Working Toward Academy Membership

Most arbitrators consider election to the National Academy to be an indication of successful work. Membership in the Academy is typically conferred on individuals with "substantial and current experience as an impartial arbitrator." Specifically, the Academy requires a minimum of five years' experience and at least fifty awards. Although the requirement has been judged as more "quantitative than qualitative,"[7] the survey responses indicate that not many individuals enter the Academy with only five years' experience. Table 4.1 indicates that the median member attained membership seven years after deciding the initial case. Thus, the criteria for admission appear to have posed a difficult hurdle for the existing members to overcome.

The criteria are also a significant hurdle for nonmembers. The median nonmember received an initial case at age 48. Assuming that the nonmembers had a comparable lag period in meeting the admission criteria, the median nonmember would be 55 before achieving membership. Because the seven-year figure represents the median, half of the nonmembers would have a longer lag period and might not enter the academy until perhaps age 60, if ever. Most people are thinking about retirement at this age rather than new careers.

Recently inducted members have been able to secure admission somewhat earlier than the median 1986 member. The author has examined the biographical data submitted by 29 applicants who were inducted during 1987 and 1988. The median age of these 29 inductees was 46, three years earlier than the median for the 1986 member. The 1987 and 1988 inductees reported that they decided their first case at age 38, four years earlier than the 1986 median member.

Probably both supply and demand factors contributed to their earlier acceptance. Individuals aspiring to become arbitrators in the 1980s may have had more information about the opportunities and training required and therefore may have been much better prepared than their predecessors twenty or thirty years ago. Moreover, the demand for new arbitrators may have resulted in the selection of these inductees. Certainly the emergence of collective bargaining in the public sector over the past generation and the widespread use of arbitration in the 1970s have aided the chances for younger individuals to achieve the same entrance requirement demanded of applicants decades ago.

Availability and the Part-time Arbitrator

Holley's chapter reported that less than half of the NAA members and only 15 percent of the nonmembers arbitrate full-time (Table 3.4). Undoubtedly a very large proportion of the arbitrators in the "entry and gaining acceptability" phase of their career practice on a part-time basis. Because it seemed likely that their principal occupation had some bearing upon their caseload, the part-time arbitrators were asked to indicate their "principal occupation" in 1986.

As might be expected, teaching and law dominated as the principal occupations of the part-time arbitrators working in 1986. About two-thirds of the respondents listed these as their primary occupations. Both teaching and law provide a great deal of flexibility in scheduling cases. This flexibility enables an individual to work at arbitration while meeting the demands of another job. Teaching may provide even more flexibility than law, accounting for the fact that over half the part-time members of the NAA listed teaching as their principal occupation.

Almost one-fifth of the part-time arbitrators (both members and non-members) indicated that their principal occupation was "retired." Undoubtedly, they had a variety of occupations before retiring. As "retired" individuals in 1986, these arbitrators could easily maintain their availability and acceptability.

Over 80 percent of the part-time arbitrators were either teachers, lawyers, or retired. The remaining part-time arbitrators included labor relations neutrals (mediators and fact-finders) and administrators in both industry and government (see Table 2.5). Undoubtedly the difficulties in maintaining availability, as well as the demands of a full-time job in government or industry, account for the very small percentage of part-time arbitrators in these occupational groupings.

To what extent do active part-time arbitrators want to work full-time? Coleman and Zirkel have reported that over 40 percent of the nonmembers in this category of arbitrators and 26 percent of the members expressed interest in working full-time (Table 2.4). The difference is significant by any conventional statistical standard. This finding suggests that part-time NAA arbitrators cannot be relied on to increase their caseload dramatically in response to demand increases. On the other hand, many nonmembers appear receptive to expanding their arbitration activities.

Phase 3: The Journeyman Years

As indicated in Bognanno's chapter on arbitration earnings, about 22 percent of the original sample reported no earnings in 1986. They were excluded from the sample that yielded information on caseloads and earnings. Almost one-fourth of the nonmembers reported that they were not working at arbitration in 1986, as compared with only 6 percent of NAA members. Moreover, one-half of the nonmembers not working in 1986 reported that they simply did not receive any cases that year, while none of the inactive members gave that reason for not working. These data indicate that NAA members are more active than nonmembers.

For most arbitrators, election into the NAA represents a new career stage. Acceptance into the Academy indicates a level of achievement—a change in status reflecting the person's caseload. Chapter 3 and Table 4.1 provide ample evidence that NAA arbitrators have decided considerably more cases in their careers and are more active currently than non-NAA arbitrators.

The NAA provides the largest proportion of full-time arbitrators. Over 40 percent of the NAA members arbitrate full-time whereas only 15 percent of the non-NAA arbitrators have achieved full-time status. The median number of cases arbitrated by the NAA members over their careers was more than ten times the median for non-NAA arbitrators (Table 4.1). Over 60 percent of the nonmembers reported fewer than 100 career cases, compared with only one percent of the members. Only seven nonmembers (about 3%) reported 1,000 or more cases, compared with 140 (about 40%) of NAA members.

NAA members are older than nonmembers and are, therefore, favored in comparing career caseloads. A comparison of caseloads in 1986 may, therefore, be more appropriate for examining comparative utilization. Only 3 percent of the non-Academy members reported sixty or more cases, compared with 29 percent of the members. Full-time NAA arbitrators reported a median caseload that more than doubled that of nonmembers—67 as opposed to 30 cases. Part-time members reported a median of thirty cases, as opposed to only five for nonmembers (Table 4.1). Bognanno shows in Chapter 6 that the NAA member charged more per case and probably heard more complex cases because the number of study days and days spent in executive session was several times the number for the non-NAA member.

It is not surprising that Academy members are utilized far more than nonmembers. They are older, better educated, and, presumably, better qualified. Moreover, the Academy's selection standards should screen out the less qualified.

The Active Nonmember

How many nonmembers have acceptability comparable to that of NAA members? The precise number is hard to estimate and is obviously dependent upon the criteria adopted, but a reasonable measure of acceptability is current caseload. As indicated above, full and part-time NAA members had median caseloads of 67 and 30, respectively, in 1986. How many nonmembers had a similar caseload?

Assuming that a nonmember is somewhat handicapped in securing appointments, a sixty-case criterion for full-time was arbitrarily established and 25 cases for part-time, nonmember arbitrators. One-third of the nonmembers who claimed full-time status (9 out of 29) met this requirement while only one-tenth of the nonmember part-time arbitrators (16 out of 164) did. Using the expansion weights to generate population estimates, these findings suggest that approximately 100 full-time and 180 part-time arbitrators with large practices in the United States do not belong to the National Academy. These 280 arbitrators would represent about forty percent of the membership of the NAA.

Why these active arbitrators do not belong to the NAA cannot be determined from the data. Some of them undoubtedly want to join but either do not have the five-year minimum required for Academy membership or their caseload is so concentrated in a few areas that they do not pass the Academy test of broad acceptability. Others, however, simply may not want to join, are bothered by the application procedure or the fees and dues, or do not feel the need.

The author has talked to one very busy nonmember arbitrator for years about joining the Academy. The individual simply responds that the application process is too much work. The author met a recent inductee at an Academy meeting and remembered that his biographical sketch had indicated that he had arbitrated hundreds of cases over many years. When asked why he waited so long to apply, he replied that he had been very busy and membership was not a high priority as long as he was busy. They may also do advocate work or belong to firms that do and therefore are ineligible for NAA membership.

Work Beyond Normal Retirement Age

Professional occupations (particularly those that permit flexible work scheduling) are known for their ability to retain older workers.[8] Arbitration provides a great deal of flexibility. Moreover, most arbitrators begin arbitrating at an advanced age and work only part-time. These factors suggest that many will want to continue working at advanced ages. The NAA data support this hypothesis and indicate further that it is the NAA member who is much more likely to work to an advanced age.

One set of respondents, which amounted to roughly 20 percent of the sample, indicated that they had retired from their principal occupation. Within this group, Academy members demonstrated a much greater willingness and ability to continue arbitrating than did the nonmembers. The "retired" nonmembers reported a median current activity level of six cases, while members reported eighteen cases. Five "retired" NAA members indicated that they had fifty or more cases in 1986, and one of these reported 129 cases! The workloads of these five arbitrators surely exceeds what most individuals would consider a part-time work commitment in retirement.

When do arbitrators stop working? The data suggest that a large number continue to work beyond age 65 and many handle heavy caseloads. For part-time arbitrators, 36 percent of the NAA members and almost a quarter of the nonmembers were over age 65. For full-time arbitrators, over one-third of the members and 17 percent of the nonmembers were over age 65. As would be expected, Academy members handled far more cases (Table 4.5).

Full-time arbitrators who belong to the NAA continue to be active in their advanced years. The median number of cases reported by full-time member arbitrators age 65 to 69 was 48. Eleven NAA members who were age 70 or over reported handling at least 30 cases in 1986, and the median number of cases was approximately 35. While these older arbitrators handle fewer cases than their younger colleagues, their caseloads are not vastly different from the figures for the entire set of full-time NAA arbitrators in 1986.

The relatively few arbitrators (3% of the arbitrator population) who responded that they were not working in 1986 because of retirement were quite old. The youngest (a nonmember) was 68, and the oldest (a member) was 86. The median age of these fully retired nonmembers was 72; for the members, 77. Almost a third of these respondents were over age 80. It is likely that some of these arbitrators retired before 1986. Nevertheless, the responses are consistent with the conclusion that arbitrators continue to work at advanced ages. An arbitrator's career at these ages may resemble that of the older trial judge. A nationwide study of American trial judges concluded that:

Though older judges (sixty-five and over) apparently choose to do less of certain tasks (especially inter-personal tasks), most differences in the work of older and younger judges are the result of court adaptations to the strengths and weaknesses of aging judges. Older judges are increasingly likely to be assigned to civil rather than criminal work and to be provided with additional resources. In addition, older judges are likely to be spared the potentially more harried non-jury trials and calendar work.[9]

Older arbitrators and older judges curtail their activities but both continue to perform some work.

The NAA survey questionnaire focused on obtaining objective data and did not attempt to obtain information regarding respondents' attitudes toward work. Therefore it is difficult to answer why some respondents continued to work well beyond age 65. Perhaps some insight can be inferred from an intensive interview study of active physicians (65 or over) that was completed about fifty years ago. The study concluded that:

In the main, the physicians realized that work had some special meaning to them, and almost all of them felt that not to work would be seriously harmful psychologically; as long as they were physically able, they continued as "doctors," either in full-time practice alone or with an assistant or as part-time practitioners or specialists.[10]

Some Issues That Apply to the Entire Career

Questions about a number of issues that were not specifically associated with a phase of the arbitral career were asked. These issues include the arbitrator's perceptions of training needs, how arbitrators feel about their caseloads, and how their caseloads develop over time.

Training Desires

Almost every career requires continuous learning to update older skills and develop new ones. This is particularly true in the case of professions, where the field often changes very rapidly. To examine this dimension of the arbitration career, the respondents were asked to identify the types of training they thought would prove beneficial over the next five years. Three blank lines followed this question to encourage the respondents to list more than one training topic.

Not all of the arbitrators wanted more training. Almost forty percent either ignored this question or indicated that no further training was desired. And of the 60 percent who answered, only one-fourth listed a second topic. But the respondents who manifested a desire for more training provided a list of more than forty topics, ranging from the very general to the very specific. Some general topics were contract interpretation, decisional thinking, and alternative dispute resolution. The more specific topics included ERISA, handicap issues, the Civil Service Reform Act of 1978, Title VII of the Civil Rights Act, and environmental arbitration. Table 4.4 provides a list of the most frequently chosen topics. The two most popular choices were not really topics but indicate the type of presentations arbitrators preferred. About one-quarter of those who listed a

Table 4.4
Self-Perceived Training Needs of Arbitrators

	Types of Training Needed in the Next Five Years (Percentages)	
	All Respondents (n = 529)	Respondents Who Listed One or More Training Needs (n = 317)
Workshops and Refresher Courses	15.4	25.1
In-Depth Training on Complex Issues	11.0	17.9
Drugs and Drug Testing	5.1	8.2
Opinion Writing	4.5	7.4
Federal Law, Federal Sector	3.9	6.4
NAA Educational Institutes	3.4	5.5
None	10.1	----
No Response	28.4	----

Expansion weights have been applied to the data.

training topic expressed a choice for "workshops; refresher courses; simulation seminars," and an additional 18 percent asked for "specific and in depth training on complex issues." There was a rapid fall-off after this, with 8 percent interested in drugs or drug testing, 7 percent in opinion writing, 6 percent in federal matters, and 5 percent in NAA educational institutes. It is safe to conclude that the educational programs for practicing arbitrators will require considerable thought and planning to be helpful.

Career Aspirations

An arbitrator's caseload is obviously a measure of success in the profession, but what arbitrators say about their caseload is a commentary on how they feel about their careers. Arbitrators who express satisfaction with their caseload or, perhaps, some desire to reduce it are indicating that they have attained their career goals. Arbitrators who express a desire for an increased caseload are indicating some dissatisfaction with their current level of achievement.

The Coleman/Zirkel chapter has already indicated that about half of the U.S. arbitrators felt that their current caseload was too small, and that it was the non-Academy members who expressed the greatest degree of dissatisfaction with their caseloads. The Holley chapter showed that the mean number of cases desired by full and part-time non-NAA members was about 55. This chapter supplements those findings, indicating that most arbitrators want to expand their practices, that nonmembers particularly want this expansion, but that their aspirations are not realistic.

Arbitrators were asked how many cases the respondents would like to have decided in 1986, and how many they would like to decide in 1987 and 1990. One possible answer was "same as now," a choice which expresses satisfaction with the caseload. The percentage of part-time and full-time member and nonmember arbitrators selecting this choice for each year is shown in the following table.

Percent of Arbitrators Expressing Satisfaction with Caseloads

Year	NAA Members	Nonmembers
	(percentages)	
1986		
Full-time	30	25
Part-time	33	11
1987		
Full-time	24	14
Part-time	24	9
1990		
Full-time	19	13
Part-time	20	7

In every case a greater proportion of NAA members expressed satisfaction with their current caseloads than nonmembers. Perhaps this satisfaction is the result of a deliberate effort by members to control their caseloads. Members have had more experience and, consequently, may have more rational expectations. Nonmembers are, of course, younger, and are seeking more experience and eventually Academy membership. Nevertheless, in 1986, one-fourth of the full-time nonmembers expressed satisfaction with their caseload, which was not strikingly different from the 30 percent response by full-time members.

Most arbitrators, however, indicated a specific number for each year. Nonmembers were amazingly consistent. The median full-time nonmembers expressed a preference for 50 cases each year, while the median part-time nonmember indicated a desire for 18 cases in both 1986 and 1987 and 23 in 1990. In view of the median caseload of thirty for full-time and five for part-time nonmember arbitrators in 1986, it can be safely concluded that these aspirations were not realized.

The median number of desired cases expressed by NAA members was much more realistic. The median number of cases desired by members, full-time and part-time, is shown in the table that follows.

Number of Cases Desired by NAA Member Arbitrators

	Full-Time	Part-Time
1986	68	30
1987	65	30
1990	50	30

These aspirations seem to be quite consistent with the median caseloads reported by members for 1986. As Holley has indicated, the average age of the NAA member is almost 60. It seems reasonable to infer that full-time NAA arbitrators intended to reduce their arbitral activities to coincide roughly with attainment of age 65. Part-time members did not, undoubtedly because many probably contemplated retiring from their principal job and expanding their arbitration practice.

In short, confirming information from earlier chapters, NAA members are much more content with their caseloads than nonmembers. Perhaps these differing levels of satisfaction result from a deliberate effort to control caseloads. It may also be related to the fact that members have more cases or that they have more experience and consequently have more rational expectations. The dissatisfaction expressed by part-time nonmember arbitrators may result from some combination of inexperience, unrealistic expectations, ambition, and lower caseloads.

Caseloads Over Time

How does an arbitrator's caseload change over time? It is impossible to answer this question fully because the respondents were not asked to provide specific information on the numbers of cases they heard at different times in their career. However, Table 4.5 provides a rough estimate.

Table 4.5
The Shape of the Arbitral Career: 1986 Grievance Cases and Age (Number of Cases)

Age	Non-NAA Members				NAA Members			
	N	Range	Mean	Median	N	Range	Mean	Median
40 or less	242	1-52	12.4	4	27	33-150	82.1	90.5
41-50	518	1-150	19.7	7	106	1-304	67.5	50
51-60	462	1-204	16.7	6	126	1-404	63.3	50
61-70	529	1-125	15.4	8	179	2-232	51.0	40
71-75	165	2-65	15.8	8	63	3-150	38.8	35
over 75	132	1-17	6.6	4.5	40	1-175	31.7	22
Totals	2,048	1-204	6	6	542	1-404	55.6	40

Expansion weights have been applied to the data.

The table shows how many cases NAA arbitrators and non-NAA arbitrators in different age brackets heard in 1986.

Considering that most arbitrators finish formal education around age 30 and spend some years in another occupation, the age bracket "40 or less" probably represents the period of "entry and gaining acceptability." For most arbitrators, particularly nonmembers, the years between ages 40 and 60 probably represent the "journeyman" years. The last two brackets, which start with age 61, seem to signal a tapering-off period.

First, the table confirms that NAA arbitrators have heavier caseloads than non-NAA arbitrators at every stage of their career. But that conclusion, while true, overlooks the fact that in each age bracket many non-NAA arbitrators handle a large number of cases. Unfortunately, the data do not allow one to determine how many are waiting for admission to the Academy or how many want to even consider applying.

Second, the table verifies once more that arbitrators work beyond normal retirement years. In 1986, about 400 U.S. arbitrators over age 70 were hearing cases, about 16 percent of the active arbitrators. Their caseloads were lower than those of younger arbitrators, but they were far from small. This suggests that the original three-stage model of the arbitral career may be inadequate. There seems to be a fourth phase which, for most arbitrators, sets in around age 60, which is marked by a long, slow decline in caseload.

Finally, the table shows that at all stages of the arbitral career there are wide variations in caseloads—arbitrators with very large caseloads and arbitrators with comparatively small ones. In every instance the mean exceeds the median. This indicates that the caseload distribution is highly skewed—in every age category there are a number of arbitrators with extremely large practices but a much larger number with much smaller practices.

Summary and Conclusions

The analysis in this chapter supports the conventional view that entry into and advancement in arbitration is difficult. The respondents to this survey reported receiving their final academic degree at about age 30. They then worked for approximately fifteen years before rendering their first award. Those who achieved Academy membership did so after an additional seven years of work, at roughly age 50. Recent inductees are receiving their first cases and entering the Academy at a much earlier age.

Teaching and law are the occupations most often designated by respondents as their principal occupations before entering arbitration, as well as the principal occupations of the part-time arbitrator. Both teaching and law enable the would-be arbitrator to have neutrality, visibility, and availability, thus enhancing the prospect of selection. Individuals with government, management, and union experience as their principal occupation are also represented among practicing arbitrators, but they are comparatively few in number and may have difficulty in gaining acceptability.

For those attaining Academy membership, there are obvious and not unexpected rewards. The caseload of members far exceeds that of nonmembers and the members expressed greater satisfaction with their caseloads. Members also indicated more realistic expectations of their future caseloads. A higher proportion of members worked beyond age 65, and some handled heavy caseloads. Clearly, many Academy members must truly enjoy their work and are quite reluctant to give it up. A small number of nonmembers are also quite successful, achieving general acceptability and working at advanced years. Why more of these nonmembers do not join the Academy is not readily apparent.

The would-be arbitrator chooses a hazardous path. A large number of people seek entry, but some are never called. Many enter the field and never build a large caseload. Most arbitrate on a part-time basis, many contentedly so, while others hope for the extra cases that will enable them to "go full-time." Finally, there is a quite small group that works at this profession full-time and makes an excellent living.

Notes

I am indebted to Gene Gallager, a colleague at the University of Kentucky, for many suggestions about career development. S. Nath, my research assistant, performed much needed computer/statistical tasks, and D. Wheeler typed many versions of this paper.

1. Douglas T. Hall, *Careers in Organizations* (Pacific Palisades, Calif.: Goodyear Publishing Company, 1976), Chapter II, pp. 16–48. See also Steven Briggs, "Arbitrators Life Cycles and Acceptability to the Parties," *Journal of Collective Negotiations in the Public Sector* 19, no. 3 (1990), pp. 189–195.

2. For a discussion of the internship program see "Report on a Survey of Labor Arbitration Interns," in *Decisional Thinking of Arbitrators and Judges*, Proceedings of the 33rd Annual Meeting of the National Association of Arbitrators (Washington: BNA Books, Inc., 1980), pp. 456–464. See also John Van N. Dorr III, "Labor Arbitrator Training: The Internship," *Arbitration Journal* 36, no. 4 (June 1981), pp. 4–10; and Arnold Zack, "Who is Responsible for the Development of Arbitrators—The Parties or the Arbitrators?" *Ibid*, pp. 11–14. For an evaluation of the success of several training programs, see Thomas J. McDermott, "Entry into Arbitration and the Effectiveness of Training Programs for Such Entry" in *Arbitration 1975*, Proceedings of the 28th Annual Meeting of the National Academy of Arbitrators (Washington: BNA Books, Inc., 1976), pp. 335–355.

3. Hall, *Careers in Organizations*, pp. 52–56.

4. Christopher A. Barreca, Anne Harmon Miller, and Max Zimny, *Labor Arbitration Development: A Handbook* (Washington: BNA Books, Inc., 1983), p. 136.

5. For a recent study of the factors in arbitrator acceptability, see Steven S. Briggs and John C. Anderson, "An Empirical Investigation of Arbitrators' Acceptability," *Industrial Relations* 19, no. 2 (1980), pp. 163–174. The study concludes that "selection frequency may be shaped by such visibility variables as professional memberships, public speaking activity, and listing in directories of arbitrators."

6. Norman Miller, Robert E. Coker, Jr., Bernard G. Greenberg, and Frances S. McConnell, "Toward A Topology of Public Health Careers," *The Milbark Memorial Fund Quarterly* XIV, no. 2 (April 1966), Part 1, pp. 201–202.

7. Ralph T. Seward, "Report of the Special Committee on Professionalism," in *Arbitration 1987: The Academy at Forty*, Proceedings of the Fortieth Annual Meeting of the National Academy of Arbitrators (Washington: BNA Books, Inc., 1988), pp. 224–225.

8. Philip L. Rones, "Employment, Earnings and Unemployment Characteristics of Older Workers," in *The Older Worker* (Madison, Wis: Industrial Relations Research Association, 1989), pp. 32–37.

9. John Paul Ryan, Alan Ashman, Bruce D. Sales, and Sandra Shane-Du Bour, *American Trial Judges* (New York: The Free Press, 1980), p. 142.

10. Eugene A. Friedman and Robert J. Havinghurst, *The Meaning of Work and Retirement* (Chicago: University of Chicago Press, 1954), p. 169.

5

The Arbitrator's Cases: Number, Sources, Issues, and Implications

Charles J. Coleman

Introduction

With this chapter attention is shifted to the arbitrator's cases. The chapter has two objectives. The first is to add a few brush strokes to the portrait of arbitration that this book has been developing. This chapter does this by describing the numbers and kinds of cases that arbitrators handle, the sources of those cases, and the principal issues involved. The chapter's second concern is the utilization of caseload information to extend many of the insights from earlier chapters on the impact of background and situational characteristics upon arbitrator activity, the effects of NAA membership, and the development of the arbitration career.

The topic of caseload is extremely important to an understanding of the arbitration profession. The number of cases decided means a great deal to arbitrators, advocates, and observers of the process. Cases have economic implications, a topic discussed in the next chapter. But being selected for cases means much more than food on the table, tuition for the children, or a luxurious vacation. The number of cases is also an indicator of acceptance within the profession, a validation of expertise, and a source of prestige. To some degree the number of cases that arbitrators decide helps to establish their credibility in the eyes of other arbitrators and their ability to influence the profession. To advocates and observers of the process, an arbitrator's caseload is often thought to be a sign of reliability and competence.

Review of Literature on Arbitral Caseloads

Arbitration Studies

There are three important sources of information about the cases that arbitrators decide. The first comes from general studies of arbitrators and of the practice of arbitration. As shown in Chapter 2 and Chapter 3, these studies frequently provide insights into the number and kinds of cases that arbitrators hear. These older studies have reported, for example, that NAA arbitrators averaged between 30 and 54 cases a year between 1952 and 1982 (Table 2.2). Following in their footsteps, Table 2.7 reports that full-time arbitrators decided a mean of approximately 65 grievances in 1986 and had handled close to 900 cases up to that point in their careers and that part-time arbitrators decided an average of 14 cases in 1986 and 210 in their careers. Table 3.8 indicates that NAA arbitrators decided an average of 56 cases in 1986 and 1,310 in their careers, while the numbers for non-NAA arbitrators were 16 and 408, respectively.

Issues

A second source of information on arbitration cases comes from inquiries into the issues decided through the arbitration process. For example, with the spread of collective bargaining throughout the public sector, a number of studies have examined the kinds of grievances that are lodged in various branches of government. These studies have shown that issues of "principle," such as arbitrability, just cause, management rights, and past practice, tend be important arbitration issues in most branches of government;[1] that the U.S. Postal Service produces an extremely large number of employee grievances, most of which involve discipline; and that leaves of absence, extra duty, evaluation processes, transfers and assignments, and job openings and postings lead the list of topics for arbitration in the schools.[2]

The published reports of the American Arbitration Association (AAA) and the Federal Mediation and Conciliation Service (FMCS) provide a great deal of empirical information on the issues addressed in their arbitration cases (Table 5.1). The pattern has been well documented over many years: discipline and discharge have long been the most frequently arbitrated issues. Almost thirty percent of AAA cases and nearly half of the FMCS cases involved employee discipline. Roughly two-thirds of the AAA disciplinary cases involved absenteeism, tardiness, physical violence, refusal of a work assignment or an order, dishonesty and theft, or alcohol and drugs. The most frequently arbitrated non-disciplinary topics were wages and fringe benefits, arbitrability, work schedules and assignments, and promotions and transfers.

Table 5.1
The Most Frequently Arbitrated Issues

The Most Frequently Arbitrated Issues (Percentages)

	AAA Jan./ Oct. 89	FMCS 1989 (Fiscal Year)
Discipline and Discharge	28.9	48.4
Wages	10.9	4.1
Arbitrability	12.4	3.4
Work Assignments & Schedules	9.4	5.2
Promotions and Transfers	11.4	3.8
Management Rights	5.9	3.4
Fringe Benefits*	6.3	8.9*
Layoff and Recall	3.4	3.9

The Most Frequently Arbitrated Disciplinary Issues (Percentages)

Absenteeism and Tardiness	21.2
Physical Violence	11.5
Refusal of Work Assignment or Order	14.8
Dishonesty and Theft	20.0
Drinking and Drugs	8.2

Source: Earl Baderschneider, Ed., Study Time: A Quarterly Letter of News and Comment for the Labor Arbitrator (New York: American Arbitration Association), No. 4, 1989. Federal Mediation and Conciliation Service, Arbitration Statistics, Fiscal Year 1989.

Including vacations, holidays, reporting pay, health and welfare, pensions, and other fringe benefits.

Activity Reports

The richest source of information about arbitration cases comes from the activity reports of appointing agencies, particularly the AAA and the FMCS. Even though the regular reports of these agencies depict only their own cases, their reports are particularly helpful here because they furnish a framework for understanding and evaluating this study's information concerning how many cases arbitrators get, who gets them, and where they come from.

Table 5.2
Arbitration Awards Issued by Arbitrators Appointed through FMCS

No. of Awards	Number of Arbitrators					
	Fiscal Year 1985	Fiscal Year 1986	Fiscal Year 1987	Fiscal Year 1988	Fiscal Year 1989	Mean for 1985-89
1	219	254	310	307	315	281.0
2 - 5	368	448	415	486	438	431.0
6 - 10	128	202	136	179	127	154.4
11 - 15	40	99	53	70	56	63.6
16 - 20	18	52	22	37	18	27.4
21 - 25	11	26	8	14	2	12.2
26 - 30	6	20	8	6	1	8.2
31 - 35	1	14	2	3	0	4.0
36 - 40	1	11	0	2	2	3.2
41 - 45	1	7	0	0	0	1.6
46 - 50	0	5	0	1	0	1.2
51 - Up	0	9	0	0	0	1.8
Total Awards	4,406	9,286	4,145	5,447	3,769	5,410.6
Number on Panel	---	1,540	---	---	---	---
Number of Arbitrators Issuing Awards	793	1,147	954	1,105	959	991
Mean Number of Awards per Arbitrator	5.6	8.1	4.3	4.9	3.9	5.5

Source: Derived from an announcement by the Federal Mediation and Conciliation Service: April 1990, supplemented with information on panel membership supplied by Jewell Myers, Director of Arbitration Services for the FMCS.

Caseloads

At the time the NAA study was conducted, the FMCS panel consisted entirely of experienced arbitrators since the threshold criterion for panel membership was five awards. Table 5.2 reports on the number of awards issued by these arbitrators in FMCS cases between 1985 and 1989. In the base year of the NAA study, 1986, there were 1,540 arbitrators on the FMCS roster[3] and 1,147 issued awards (about 74% of the panel). The mean number of FMCS awards issued by panel arbitrators *who had at least one FMCS case* was about eight and the mean for all arbitrators on the panel was six.

But 1986 may have been an unusually busy year for arbitrators on the FMCS panel. The figure of almost 9,300 awards for that year was more than double the average for the other four years. Over the entire five-year period, an average of slightly fewer than 1,000 arbitrators issued awards in FMCS cases each year—roughly 65 percent of the 1986 panel membership and less than 60 percent of the 1990 panel membership. In these years, the mean number of awards for all arbitrators with at least one award was less than five, and the mean number of awards for all arbitrators on the FMCS panel was closer to three.

Table 5.2 also illustrates the recent decline in FMCS arbitration cases. The 1989 figure of 3,769 awards represented a five-year low. It was 30 percent below the average for the five years and almost 60 percent below the peak attained in 1986. This decline is reflected in AAA caseloads as well, which reached a peak of 19,218 filings for labor arbitration cases in 1987 and then fell to 15,719 in 1989 (a decline of 18%).[4]

A Skewed Distribution

Table 5.2 also shows that a small percentage of arbitrators do most of the business. During each of the five years reported on the table, roughly one-third of the arbitrators on the FMCS panel heard no cases at all. In 1986, one-quarter of the 1,540 arbitrators on the panel (393 arbitrators) did not hear a single FMCS case, and 46 percent (702 arbitrators) heard one or two cases. At the other extreme, roughly 4 percent (66 arbitrators) heard more than 25 FMCS cases and 16 percent heard more than ten cases (243 arbitrators).[5]

The skewed nature of the distribution of FMCS cases is illustrated in Figure 5.1. The chart depicts the number of FMCS cases decided by those arbitrators who had one or more FMCS cases in the base year of the NAA study. The percentage of cases decided is shown on the vertical axis and the percentage of arbitrators deciding them, on the horizontal axis. Testifying to the skewed nature of case distribution, the figure shows that, at one extreme, the busiest 10 percent of the arbitrators decided more than 30 percent of the FMCS cases while the least busy 10 percent decided about 1 percent.

Sources of Cases: Sector and Industry

What are the industries or the part of the economy that rely most heavily on arbitration? The FMCS provides a public/private sector breakdown of cases. Taking the most recent period of time (1988 and 1989), arbitrators operating under FMCS auspices issued 9,216 awards. Almost 85 percent of these arbitration cases came from the private sector; slightly less than

Figure 5.1
Arbitration Case Loads (1986)

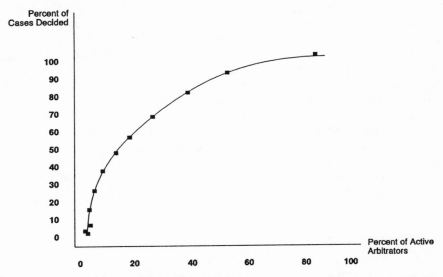

Source: Part of a study presented to the Board of Governors and the National Academy of
        Arbitrators by Clifford E. Smith, February 1988.

10 percent involved the federal government (870 cases); and 6 percent (559 cases) came from some other part of the public sector.[6]

The FMCS statistics greatly understate the number and proportion of public sector cases that come to arbitration because most state and municipal cases are administered through either state panels or the American Arbitration Association. Relatively speaking, the AAA data may provide a more realistic picture of the public/private sector case breakdown. Traditionally, about 56 percent of AAA cases came from the private sector and 44 percent from the public sector. But that percentage has been shifting toward the public sector in recent years. In 1988 and 1990, roughly 51 percent of the AAA cases originated in the private sector and 49 percent in some branch of government or public education.[7]

The AAA also reports its cases by industry, and Table 5.3 provides that information for the years that bracket the base year for the NAA study. Roughly half of the private sector cases are in manufacturing, with a substantial number of cases in service and trade, and health care. In the public sector, almost half of the grievances involve teachers (although this percentage appeared to be declining around the time of the NAA study), and a fair number of cases come out of law enforcement. The large and growing "other" category comes from non-uniformed employees of federal, state, county, or municipal government.

Table 5.3
Arbitration Awards by Industry

	Aug. 1984 Aug. 1985	Jan. 1987 Oct. 1987
Private Sector	(Percentages)	
Manufacturing	59.2	48.8
Office	.8	1.1
Professional	1.9	1.4
Service & Trade	21.0	15.8
Transportation	5.4	3.9
Health Care	4.3	15.2
Other	7.6	13.9
Public Sector		
Teachers	55.0	38.2
Police	8.7	9.7
Fire Fighters	5.2	5.8
Health Care	13.2	10.9
Other	17.8	35.5

Source: Earl Baderschneider, Ed., Study Time: A Quarterly Letter of News and Comment for the Labor Arbitrator (New York: American Arbitration Association), April 1986, No. 4, 1988, and No. 4, 1989.

Results of the NAA Study

Arbitrators do many things: they resolve grievances involving unionized and non-unionized employees; they hear interest disputes; they become involved in mediation, mediation-arbitration (med-arb), and fact-finding; and they do some work in the field of alternative dispute resolution. Table 5.4 uses the data from the NAA study to estimate the overall level of activity of members of the arbitration profession in the United States.[8] Remember that this table was constructed from data supplied by *arbitrators who had decided at least one case in 1986.* Just as the FMCS and the AAA reported that a large number of arbitrators on their rosters do not decide any cases, more than 20 percent of the arbitrators in the NAA

Table 5.4
Profile of Arbitral Activity (1986)

Grievance and Interest Cases	Percentage with Cases*	Mean Number of Cases*	Median Number of Cases*	Total Cases*
		(Population Figures for Active Arbitrators with Cases)		
Grievance	98.7	24.4	10	64,636 (80.8%)
Nor union	17.6	4.1	2	1,916
Interest	33.3	3.7	2	3,320
Other Cases				
Mediation	23.6	5.9	4	3,748
Med-arb	14.5	7.7	4	2,898
Fact-finding	20.6	3.6	2	2,004
ADR (paid)	8.7	6.4	2	1,493
Components of ADR Activity				
Commercial	4.8	4.6	3	596
Community	3.0	2.0	2	159
Inter-corporation	Neg.	--	--	33
Environmental	Neg.	--	--	10
Family	2.2	2.2	2	129
Court Annexed	3.6	4.1	2	392
Other	3.5	2.0	1	184
	Total Grievance and Interest Cases			69,872
	Total Other Cases			10,143
	Grand Total			80,015

Expansion weights have been applied to these data. Five of the 529 active arbitrators reported having no grievance cases in 1986 (but heard other cases). If the inactive arbitrators were added to the list, the percentage of arbitrators who had decided grievances   would fall to 84.5 percent.

study did not decide a single case in 1986 and are not included in the analysis here and in most other parts of this book.

In 1986, almost 99 percent of the active U.S. arbitrators decided at least one grievance case involving a unionized employee, and 17 percent heard a non-union grievance. One-third of the active arbitrators heard at least one interest case; between 20 and 25 percent became involved in mediation or fact-finding; and 15 percent participated in med-arb cases. Although much is written today about the emerging field of Alternative Dispute Resolution (ADR), a comparatively small percentage of arbitrators took on cases involving such matters as commercial arbitration, community disputes, inter-corporation matters, environmental or family concerns, or court-annexed cases.

The mean for grievances involving unionized employees was 24 cases and the median was ten. Those arbitrators who had interest cases or cases involving non-union employees had about four of each; those that did some mediation had around a half-dozen cases; those who became involved in med-arb cases had about eight; the arbitrators who received fact-finding cases had nearly four. Less than 10 percent of the arbitrators performed any ADR work but for those who did, the mean number of cases was 6.4 and the median was two.

In 1986, labor arbitrators decided almost 70,000 grievance and interest cases and handled roughly 10,000 non-arbitration assignments, including ADR cases. More than 80 percent of the activity involved the grievances of unionized employees. No other category commanded as much as 5 percent of the overall caseload.

Sources of Cases

Grievance assignments come to arbitrators from many directions, and Table 5.5 summarizes the survey data on the sources of grievances. More than half of the U.S. arbitrators received grievance cases from the AAA or the FMCS in 1986, with the typical arbitrator deciding an average of about half-a-dozen cases from each agency. Roughly 40 percent of arbitrators were picked for cases directly by the parties, with the mean number being slightly less than eight. State agencies provided a mean of six cases, but only one-third of the arbitrators received cases from these agencies.

Two particularly fruitful sources of cases were permanent panels and permanent umpireships, but comparatively few arbitrators participated. Almost 30 percent of arbitrators received cases as a result of a panel membership, with an average of sixteen cases. Less than one arbitrator in ten had a permanent umpireship, but the umpires received an average of twelve cases from that source in 1986.

Although the number of interest arbitration cases is dwarfed by the number of grievances, a few words should be devoted to interest cases. This form of arbitration is primarily a phenomenon of those public sector jurisdictions that have passed an interest arbitration law. Interest arbitration is an optional method of contract dispute resolution in the federal government, and it is specified as the terminal step in contract impasse proceedings in the U.S. Postal Service. Interest arbitration laws also cover public employees in some 25 states. Most of those laws give public safety employees the right to take unresolved contract disputes to arbitration, but some states extend the right to municipal employees, teachers, transit workers, or to larger groups of state, county, or municipal employees.[9]

Because the bulk of interest arbitration cases involve public sector non-

Table 5.5
Sources of Cases (1986)

Agency	Percent with Cases*	Mean Number of Cases*	Median Number of Cases*	Sum of 1986 Cases
	(Population Figures for Active Arbitrators with Cases)			
	Grievance Cases			
FMCS	55.4	7.0	4.0	10,445
AAA	56.5	6.5	2.0	9,906
Direct Appointment	42.4	7.7	4.0	8,780
State Agency	34.9	6.0	3.0	5,636
Permanent Panel	29.5	15.8	8.0	12,555
Permanent Umpireship	9.1	12.0	5.0	2,935
Other	5.9	7.9	3.0	1,256
				51,513
	Interest Cases			
FMCS	5.1	2.5	2.1	344
AAA	6.0	1.8	1.0	286
Direct Appointment	6.6	2.3	1.0	406
State Agency	16.6	4.1	2.0	1,805
Permanent Panel	1.5	5.2	4.0	205
Permanent Umpireship	0.5	2.5	2.0	35
Other	0.4	1.9	2.0	22
				2,702

* Expansion weights have been applied to these data.

federal employees, it is not surprising to find that most interest arbitration cases come to arbitrators through state agencies. In 1986, 17 percent of the arbitrators received a mean of 4.1 cases from state agencies set up to administer a public employee labor relations statute. Close to 7 percent of arbitrators received at least one interest case directly from the parties, and about 6 percent secured about two cases apiece from the AAA or FMCS. Only a handful of arbitrators received cases from permanent panels, umpireships, or other sources.

Some Words About These Numbers

These are probably the first empirically based estimates that have ever been made of the total caseload of U.S. arbitrators, the kinds of cases they hear, and where those cases come from. The information reported in the tables came from Questions 26 and 27 in the NAA questionnaire (see Appendix I). Both questions asked arbitrators to specify the number of grievance/interest cases involving a union or employer association and the sources of these cases.

The data that are reported in these tables have outside support and are, basically, internally consistent. In the few instances where there is external information on arbitration cases, the numbers that have been reported are quite close to those in these tables. For example, Table 5.2 reported that in 1986, arbitrators issued almost 9,300 awards in FMCS cases and endnote 5 placed the number of AAA awards for that year at approximately 9,000. The numbers reported in Table 5.5 are within 10 percent of those figures.

As far as internal consistency is concerned, the total number of grievances from different sources reported in Table 5.5 is roughly three-quarters of the total number of grievances reported in Table 5.4, and the number of interest arbitration cases in Table 5.5 is 81 percent of that reported in Table 5.4. But much of the difference is accounted for by arbitrators who provided an overall case estimate but did not provide a breakdown by appointing sources. Approximately 10 percent of the sample failed to answer the breakdown question. These arbitrators decided 12 percent of the grievances and 4 percent of the interest cases. If their cases were added to the totals on Table 5.6, that table would account for almost 92 percent of the grievances and 85 percent of the interest cases.

What is surprising about Table 5.6 concerns the role played by FMCS and AAA in arbitral caseloads. The commonly held belief is that these two agencies dominate the field, but they appear to be involved in only about 40 percent of the cases. The number of cases that they process is roughly equivalent to the number that arbitrators receive directly either through panel memberships (the largest number on the table) or direct selection. State agencies and permanent umpireships handle about 17 percent of the cases.

The Skewed Distribution

Reflecting data reported earlier in this chapter, the cases were distributed unevenly. A comparatively small number of arbitrators handled most of the cases. Table 5.6 shows that the least active 25 percent of the arbitrators heard only 2 percent of the cases; the less active 50 percent decided about 10 percent of the cases (with none of these hearing more

Table 5.6
Distribution of Grievance Cases (1986)

Arbitrators*	(Percentages) Grievance Cases*	Number of Grievance Cases
15.7	1.0	0-1
24.3	2.0	0-3
52.4	9.3	0-10
68.0	19.1	0-20
75.2	26.4	0-28
88.8	50.0	0-58
100	100	0-404

* Expansion weights have been applied to these data.

than ten cases); and the busiest 10 percent of the U.S. arbitrators decided about half of the 1986 cases.

Industries and Issues

The NAA questionnaire also asked the respondents to list the industries that gave them the largest number of cases and the issues that came to them. There are few surprises in the these areas because the information from the survey mirrors the data reported in our survey of the literature. Fifty-six percent of the grievance arbitration cases were private sector in origin and most of these cases came from the long-standing strongholds of the union movement—manufacturing, food processing, transportation, pulp and paper, and steel. Forty-four percent of the grievance cases that came to arbitration in 1986 came from the public sector. The chief sources of public sector grievances are school districts, municipal and state governments, and the federal government in that order.

Table 5.7 portrays the issues that most frequently came to arbitration in 1986. The respondents were given a list of 42 grievance topics, arranged alphabetically from absenteeism to working conditions. They were then asked to encircle the three issues they had decided most frequently in 1986. Reflecting previously reported AAA and FMCS information, discharge heads the list of arbitration topics. Almost 72 percent of the arbitrators heard at least one discharge case in 1986—almost as many arbitrators heard discharge cases as heard the thirty least arbitrated issues combined. Matters relating to discipline such as absenteeism and work performance came in second and third place, and almost 40 percent had

Table 5.7
The Most Frequently Decided Issues (1986)

Item	Number of Times Listed		Percent of Arbitrators Hearing Issue[*]
	Sample	Population[*]	
Discharge	412	1,875	71.8
Absenteeism	144	589	22.6
Work Performance	67	401	15.4
Management Rights	86	386	14.8
Seniority	84	345	13.7
Past Practice	75	340	13.0
Layoff/Bumping/Recall	66	334	12.8
Wage/Salary/ Compensation	55	307	11.8
Assignment of Work	58	293	11.2
Arbitrability	65	285	10.9
Job Posting/Bidding	35	226	8.6
Alcohol and Drug Abuse	31	155	5.9
Other (30 issues)	296	1,903	72.9

[*] Expansion weights have been applied to these data.

heard one or both of these issues. These topics were followed by such standard contractual issues as management rights, seniority, past practice, and employment issues. These were followed by wage and salary issues, work assignment, arbitrability, job posting and bidding, and alcohol and drug abuse.

Impact of Background and Situational Variables

This chapter had two objectives: the first was to help complete the portrait of arbitration that this book has been developing, and the second was the utilization of caseload information to extend a number of insights from earlier chapters. Of particular interest was the impact of background and situational characteristics upon arbitrator activity, the effects of NAA membership on caseload, and caseload levels in the context of the arbi-

Table 5.8
The Significant Correlates of Caseload (1987)

Background Variables		Organizations		Non-Agency Appointments	
Law Degree	.11**	AAA	.27***	Panel Memberships	.44***
Age	.08**	IRRA	.18***	Postal Panel	.34***
Experience	.19***	SPIDR	.21***	Steel Panel	.14***
		FLRP	.24***	Other Panels	.25***
		Labor Law	.13**	Perm. Ump.	.40***
		NAA	.55***	Direct	.59***
		Other Societies	-.26***		

Caseload Variables		Aspirations	
Interest Cases	.31**	Number of 1987 Cases	.21***
Non-Union	.24***		
Mediation	.13**	Number of 1990 Cases	.18***
Med-Arb	.12**	Cases Refused	.37***
ADR (Paid)	.11**		
Cases in Career	.65***		

*p ≤ .05
**p ≤ .01
***p ≤ .001

tration career. Up to this point, attention has been focused on the first objective. Now it turns to the second.

Table 5.8 lists the variables that demonstrated a statistically significant relationship with the number of grievances reported by the respondents in 1986, the correlation coefficients, and the level of significance. Five different kinds of variables show up in this table. One set ties into the arbitrator's background, but these relationships were infrequent and they were not strong. The current caseload was found to be positively related to the possession of a law degree (lawyers get more cases) and to two time-related items (the older and more experienced arbitrators get more cases).

The relationships between the current caseload and membership in several professional societies was consistently positive and somewhat more pronounced. Placing some of the results from the Coleman-Zirkel chapter into a caseload context, the busier arbitrators were active in professional labor relations societies, including the NAA, but they did not join many other organizations. Busy arbitrators apparently organize much of their lives around their arbitration practice and devote comparatively little attention elsewhere. The busy arbitrator also receives cases from a much wider variety of sources—particularly from panel memberships, permanent umpireships, and direct appointments.

The table also shows that all of the elements in the caseload are tied together. The arbitrator who is busy with the grievances of unionized employees also tends to have a heavier than average load of non-union grievances, interest cases, mediation, med-arb, fact-finding, and ADR assignments.

The table also demonstrates how the present is built upon the past. The variable that is most strongly related to current arbitral activity is past activity. The current caseload apparently is, to a large degree, a function of acceptability and trust won through previous service. Finally, the table shows that busy arbitrators want to be busy. Even though they are the most active people in the field, they refuse fewer cases and they express a desire to expand their practice even further in the future.

It should be remembered that conclusions drawn from a relatively small set of correlation coefficients must be considered tentative. The findings essentially provide a set of insights that should be tested and refined in later research by applying more sophisticated tools to more specific information. However, with this caveat in mind, taken as a whole, a number of background and situational characteristics appear to be related to the arbitrator's caseload. Early life variables such as the level and kind of education do not appear to be as important as age, length of experience, prior success, participation in activities that lend professional visibility, and the desire for more cases.

The connecting link may be information shortages (a point which will be developed in the next chapter). The advocates selecting arbitrators want competence, an impartial hearing, and determinations grounded in the merits of the case. But their information on arbitrators is less than perfect. When they make a selection, therefore, the quantity of information that they have on the arbitrator becomes extremely important. They would lean to the arbitrator they know (perhaps from a professional society) over the one they don't know. They would normally prefer the oldtimer or the arbitrator with a large client base because their track record will be better known. When dealing with interest cases, med-arb, panel selection, umpireships, and non-arbitral activity (such as mediation or fact-finding), the selector leans toward the arbitrator whose track record has been established through a large grievance practice.

The NAA Effect

Most of the people who are familiar with arbitration think that NAA membership has a positive effect on an arbitrator's caseload. While there is a great deal of evidence in this book and in other studies that NAA members are much busier than nonmembers, the causal link between membership and cases is very difficult to establish. There is a "which came first, the chicken or the egg" problem here. Is NAA membership simply a result of an already heavy caseload or does it create an enlarged caseload?

This question cannot be answered definitively from the analysis conducted for this chapter. The survey did not gather longitudinal data showing how the caseloads of arbitrators developed over time and how the number of cases changed after admission to the Academy. Thus, it is impossible to determine directly whether an arbitrator's caseload changed shortly after the achievement of Academy membership, and there is an even more tenuous basis for speculating about how caseload would change if a nonmember were admitted to NAA. But the caseloads of groups of arbitrators at different stages of their careers can be examined to develop some tentative answers about whether NAA membership seems to lead to more cases or whether membership is simply an effect of an already heavy caseload.

The analysis of the NAA impact is built around the data presented in Table 5.9 and in Figure 5.2. Four classes of arbitrators are represented in the table: full and part-time arbitrators who belong to the NAA, and full and part-time arbitrators who do not belong. The full-time arbitrators who are not NAA members are *not* analyzed in detail and they are not depicted in Figure 5.2 for two reasons.

First, comparatively few respondents fell into this category—only 26 respondents were full-time arbitrators but not NAA members. When the arbitrators were later divided on the basis of different levels of experience, the cell sizes became very small. It seemed fruitless to attempt drawing conclusions from ten cells of data when three were blank, and six contained information gathered from only one to five respondents. Second, it is probable that a very large proportion of these arbitrators were on the verge of Academy membership. The NAA requires a minimum of five years' arbitration experience. Nineteen of these arbitrators (73%) had seven or fewer years of experience and, thus, they were just coming into

Table 5.9
Median Number of Cases Decided by Years of Experience (1986)

Years of Experience	FT/NAA	FT/Non-NAA	PT/NAA	PT/Non-NAA
1	0	3 (n = 1)	0	2 (n = 9)
2-3	0	8 (n = 1)	0	3 (n = 13)
4-5	0	50 (n = 5)	0	4 (n = 17)
6-10	67 (n = 22)	24 (n = 13)	35 (n = 10)	5 (n = 45)
11-15	77 (n = 33)	125 (n = 1)	27 (n = 42)	8 (n = 35)
16-20	80 (n = 25)	62.5 (n = 4)	30 (n = 45)	7 (n = 16)
21-25	79 (n = 16)	0	27.5 (n = 26)	6 (n = 7)
26-30	62 (n = 18)	0	35 (n = 18)	5 (n = 10)
31-40	42.5 (n = 22)	0	23 (n = 31)	7 (n = 10)
>40	77.5 (n = 8)	17 (n = 1)	22 (n = 16)	1 (n = 1)
Total	66 (n = 144)	31 (n = 26)	30 (n = 188)	5 (n = 163)
Percent of Population (Expansion Weights Used)	9.0 (n = 238)	10.9 (n = 286)	11.8 (n = 311)	68.3 (n = 1795)

FT = Full-time
PT = Part-time

that time in their careers when NAA membership was a realistic possibility.

Part-time, Nonmembers

The part-time arbitrators who had not been admitted to the Academy had very small arbitration practices no matter what their level of experience. In 1986, the median arbitrator in this group with five years of

Figure 5.2
Current Caseload and Years of Experience (Median Caseloads)

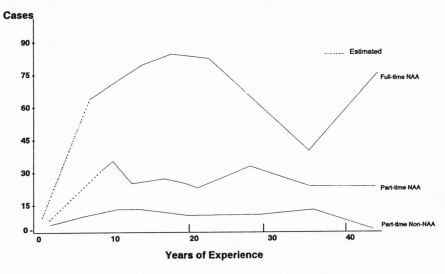

experience heard four cases; with ten years, five cases; with fifteen years, eight cases; and with more years of experience, five to seven cases. The number of cases heard by this group of part-time arbitrators, therefore, builds quite slowly through the early years of their careers, reaches a crest of about eight cases a year between the tenth and the fifteenth year, and slowly declines for a decade or more until the number of cases almost vanishes. Their careers are substantially different from the careers of those arbitrators who are elected to the Academy. Unfortunately, almost seventy percent of the arbitrators who were active in 1986 fell into this category.

Part-time, Members

Because NAA membership requires a minimum of five years of arbitration experience, there are no entries for NAA members with fewer than five years of arbitration experience. But the results show that by the time today's NAA members had logged six to ten years in arbitration, they had already developed a sizable caseload. The least experienced group of NAA-member, part-time arbitrators averaged 35 cases a year by the time they had six to ten years in the field. Arbitrators in the same category with more experience, however, continued to average 30 to 35 cases a year until very late in their career. Then, sometime after their thirtieth year in arbitration, their caseload began to decline, dropping to about 20 cases a year.

Full-time, Members

Turning finally to the NAA members who arbitrated full-time, the arbitrators with six to ten years' experience were handling a median of almost 70 cases a year. The number of cases decided by their full-time colleagues with 11 to 25 years of experience was in the high seventies or low eighties. Arbitrators with more years of experience reported progressively fewer cases except for a small group of very senior, but apparently quite vigorous arbitrators, who hear a median of close to 80 cases after 40 years in the field.

The NAA Effect?

Does NAA membership have an effect on caseloads? Despite the ample evidence showing that NAA arbitrators are much busier than their non-Academy colleagues, the answer to this question is not clear. These findings certainly suggest that it is the first five years or so in arbitration—the years prior to NAA membership—that are critical to caseloads. By the sixth year or so, the future caseload level appears to be fairly well established. Most who have not "made it" by that time probably never will.

In addition, these data indicate that the arbitrators who ultimately enter the NAA separate themselves from the rest of the pack very early in their careers. Compare, for example, the caseload patterns of part-time NAA and non-NAA arbitrators. By the time those who enter the Academy become eligible for membership, most already have substantial caseloads. In this sense, NAA membership seems to be an effect rather than a cause of cases.

But the answer is not as simple as that. A great deal seems to depend on whether the individual arbitrates part-time or full-time. NAA members with six to ten years of experience averaged 35 cases a year if they arbitrated part-time, and 67 if full-time. But the median number of cases for the part-time arbitrators remained roughly the same with higher levels of experience, while the median for full-time arbitrators rose to approximately 80 and stayed there for a decade and a half. The caseloads of the full-time arbitrators, therefore, grew by perhaps fifteen to 20 percent after membership.[10]

It appears that the busy part-time arbitrators may have some kind of caseload objective—a load which permits them to balance their arbitration practice with the demands of their primary occupation. Many apparently reach this level by the time they become eligible for membership in the

Academy and then take the steps necessary to curtail further growth in their arbitration practice.[11] Full-time arbitrators, however, may have the time, the inclination, and perhaps the need for more cases and NAA membership may be of some assistance in securing them. That NAA membership may have some positive impact on caseloads for those who want their practice to continue growing is entirely possible. A related point is that some parties request only NAA members from the appointing agencies.

Speculations about Cases and the Arbitral Career

The data suggest that at least three subpopulations of arbitrators exist in the United States today. The Coleman/Zirkel and Krislov chapters have already shown that arbitration is a career that people enter after they have done something else for many years. Most arbitrators probably begin their careers by arbitrating part-time. It takes some time to build an arbitration practice. Thus, they teach, consult, or practice law while their caseload builds. Some of these arbitrators probably have full-time arbitration as a goal from the time they prepare for their first case.

The first subpopulation of arbitrators may consist of those arbitrators who succeed in making the transition to a full-time practice. Although some may enter the full-time ranks after retiring from another occupation, many of these seem to be comparatively young arbitrators whose caseloads have developed quite rapidly. Within five years or so they have a load of perhaps fifty or more cases a year. Almost all of these arbitrators enter the Academy, and most of those who had not done so when the survey was conducted, probably entered once they met the experience requirements.

The second subpopulation consists of arbitrators who have fairly large practices—maybe twenty to fifty cases a year—but who do not abandon their primary occupation until perhaps they retire from it. Most of these arbitrators belong to the NAA. Some of them are undoubtedly content with arbitration as a part-time vocation, as is probably the case with many arbitrators who are also university professors. Within this group, as Krislov has reported in Chapter 4, there are probably a fair number who would like to arbitrate full-time, but their practice has not yet reached (and may never reach) a level that permits them to do so. But there are also a fair number whose retirement income may reduce their economic incentive to actively seek cases.

But the data also suggest that there is a third subpopulation: perhaps a persistent underclass. The members of this subpopulation always remain in the part-time ranks, some perhaps by choice but others by necessity. Their caseloads never reach the level required for NAA membership and they never generate the income that would permit them to "go full-time." Undoubtedly some of the people in this category leave the field. Others probably treat arbitration as a part-time job and a secondary source of funds. But within this set of arbitrators there is probably a group that feels condemned to Thoreau's life of "quiet desperation." They want more cases, may want them desperately, and they feel some pain or resentment every time they compare themselves to their more active colleagues.

Summary and Conclusions

In 1986, U.S. arbitrators dealt with about 65,000 employee grievances, more than 3,000 interest disputes, and roughly 10,000 related procedures (such as mediation or fact-finding). Employee grievances are at the heart of the arbitration practice but these grievances are distributed unevenly: 10 percent of the arbitrators decide about 50 percent of the cases while the least busy 25 percent decide only 2 percent of the cases.

Arbitrators receive their cases from many sources. Many of the arbitrators receive a substantial part of their grievance cases through the AAA or the FMCS, while most assignments of interest cases come from state agencies. The busiest arbitrators, however, draw much more heavily on direct selection by the parties, permanent panel memberships, or permanent umpireships for their cases. Arbitrators deal with many questions as they hear their cases, but matters of discharge and discipline head the list of issues decided.

The arbitrator's caseload does not seem to be as strongly related to personal background as it does to activity in professional associations, the ability to get assigned to panels and umpireships, and the desire to expand caseload. Arbitration is not a vocation for the bashful. Selection for cases in one kind of arbitration leads to selection in related areas. The arbitrator busy with grievance cases appears to receive more interest cases, more mediation, more med-arb assignments, more fact-finding, and perhaps more ADR work than the less active grievance arbitrator.

The data do not provide a completely clear answer to the question of whether NAA membership leads to an increase in cases. The arbitrators who are elected to the Academy typically have large caseloads before their admission. The practices of part-time arbitrators do not seem to grow after achieving membership, but the practices of full-time arbitrators do expand by perhaps fifteen to twenty percent. This finding suggests that NAA membership can help expand the caseload of the arbitrator who wants it to be expanded.

Notes

1. Charles J. Coleman, "Grievance Arbitration in the Public Sector: Status, Issues, and Problems," *Journal of Collective Negotiations in the Public Sector* 16 (1987), pp. 37–52.

2. Frank R. Annunziato, "Grievance Arbitration in Connecticut: K–12 Public Education," *The Arbitration Journal* 42, no. 3 (Sept. 1987), pp. 46–57; D. W. Brodie and P. A. Williams, *School Grievance Arbitration* (Seattle, Wash.: Butterworth, 1982).

3. Information supplied by Jewell L. Myers, Director of FMCS Arbitration Services, March 1991. By 1990 the number of arbitrators on the FMCS panel had grown to 1,722.

4. Information supplied by Earl Baderschneider, editor of Labor Publications for the American Arbitration Association (AAA), March and November 1991. The AAA no longer keeps records of awards issued each year, but it keeps records of cases filed. Between 1985 and 1990, the average number of cases filed each year was 17,645. In the base year of our study, 1986, 18,335 cases were filed. When the AAA kept records of awards issued (through the early 1980s), in almost every year somewhere between 48 percent and 52 percent of case filings resulted in awards. This suggests that in 1986 the arbitration population decided between 8,800 and 9,500 AAA cases.

5. An even smaller percentage of arbitrators on the AAA panel decide cases. Between 1986 and 1989 there were approximately 3,000 arbitrators listed on this panel. In each of these years an average of 1,068 arbitrators, or about 36 percent decided one or more cases. Information supplied by Earl Baderschneider, editor of the AAA publication *Study Time*.

6. Federal Mediation and Conciliation Service Arbitration Statistics, Fiscal Year 1988 and 1989, supplied by Jewell L. Myers, FMCS Director of Arbitration Services.

7. Earl Baderschneider, ed., *Study Time*, #4, 1988 and #1, 1990 (New York: American Arbitration Association). The 1990 figures came from a personal conversation with Mr. Baderschneider in March 1991.

8. It should be remembered that, while the means and medians in this and other tables in this chapter are single figure or point estimates, those numbers are really representative of a range. Rather than burden the reader with additional statistical measures (the standard deviation) representing the range, only the point estimate is provided.

9. Charles J. Coleman, *Managing Labor Relations in the Public Sector* (San Francisco: Jossey-Bass, Inc., 1990), p. 225.

10. Although I take full responsibility for this analysis of the NAA impact, I want to thank one of the co-authors of this volume, Joseph Krislov, for pointing out why my original (and now abandoned) reading of the data was entirely wrong.

11. For example, by withdrawing from the AAA or FMCS panels temporarily, when the caseload demands conflict too heavily with other occupational demands.

6

Feast or Famine: Critical Differences in Arbitration Earnings

Mario F. Bognanno

Introduction

Annual earnings from labor arbitration averaged $25,574 in 1986. This estimate was not well received by students of mine aspiring to careers as arbitrators. This reaction was not surprising. After all, in that same year, our newly minted students with M.A. degrees in Industrial Relations earned about $30,000.

"How on earth," one student asked, "can such an 'average' salary justify the time and expense of becoming an arbitrator?" "Good question," I replied. But cutting off my response, another student asked: "How much did part-time arbitrators make, particularly those who do not belong to the National Academy of Arbitrators (NAA)?" Answer: $10,634. "That's awful," she murmured. "True, but those arbitrators earned only about 20 percent of their gross income from neutral work in 1986," I responded. Then my favorite pupil inquired: "What were average earnings for NAA and non-NAA arbitrators who work at it full-time?" Answer: $98,850 and $44,499, respectively.

My students' shaken perceptions about earnings from the practice of labor arbitration are significant. The fact is that perennially some arbitrators do quite well while others do not, and this can be a difficult lesson to learn. Another difficult lesson—as told by Krislov in Chapter 4—is that it usually takes several years to become established as a labor arbitrator. Even more seasoned individuals choosing to try their hand at arbitration often act on the basis of incomplete, even incorrect, information about earnings. Over the years, I have conferred with many mediators, labor relations managers, business agents, and attorneys who were contemplating career changes. More often than not, I was amazed at how little they knew about the distribution of arbitration earnings.

Information about earnings from labor arbitration practices in the United States is not widely available, particularly in comparison to earnings data that are available for other much larger and, generally, full-time professions like medicine, law, and education. The purpose of this chapter is to analyze and present information about the 1986 earnings of practicing labor arbitrators in the United States and, in doing so, partially fill this information gap. While it is true that the level of arbitration earnings may change with time, this does not imply that the distribution character of earnings is nearly as time-sensitive. From year to year there is doubtless little change (1) in the proportion of practicing arbitrators in the bottom and top brackets of the earnings distribution, (2) in the ratio of full-time to part-time arbitration earnings or NAA to non-NAA arbitration earnings, or (3) in the marginal relationship between annual earnings and career cases decided. Thus, a great deal can be learned about the long-term character of earnings from a simple annual cross-section analysis.

In addition to their earnings from grievance and interest arbitration, most labor arbitrators receive retirement income or earnings from teaching or practicing law. Furthermore, many labor arbitrators work as mediators, fact-finders, non-union grievance arbitrators, or neutrals in other dispute resolution settings. However, incomes and earnings from the above sources are not the subject of this analysis. This chapter's inquiry is limited to the study of earnings from the arbitration of union-management disputes: specifically, the earnings that flow to labor arbitrators for deciding grievance and interest disputes.

From the classroom exchanges mentioned above, my students learned that there are different "averages" that can be constructed from earnings data. This chapter's special focus is on *average* earnings categorized by "membership status" (i.e., whether an NAA member or nonmember) and "work status" (i.e., whether working full or part-time as a labor arbitrator). Attention is also called to differences in earnings between men and women arbitrators.

Although data exist on per diem fees and revenue per case, this may be the first examination of earnings from the practice of labor arbitration in the United States. Consequently, the information reported here may become the baseline against which subsequent research on arbitration earnings may be compared. Thus, a caveat is warranted about the interpretation given to the earnings information reported in this chapter.

Chapter 1, Table 1.2, and Chapter 2 called attention to the fact that roughly one-fifth of those listed in 1987 national, regional, state and/or local arbitration agency directories did not decide a single arbitration case

Table 6.1
Grievance Cases (1986)

Variables	non-NAA	NAA	Total[1]
Grievance Decisions[***]	15.97 (193)[2]	55.65 (336)	24.37 (529)
Work Status[***]			
Full-time[**]	49.37 (30)	82.99 (146)	63.77 (176)
Part-time[***]	9.83 (163)	34.64 (190)	13.61 (353)

[1] Weighted averages use 11.0114 and 1.6536 to weight non-NAA and NAA observations, respectively.

[2] Number of observations in parentheses.

[**] Difference is statistically significant at $\alpha = .01$; [***] at $\alpha = .001$ (two-tailed tests).

in 1986. Consequently, these individuals reported zero earnings from arbitration and they are not included in the present analysis.

Only arbitrators who decided at least one case in 1986 are considered here. Omitting the others arguably *biases upward* average earning calculations. Thus, to play it safe, this chapter's findings probably should not be generalized beyond the population of American arbitrators who were active in 1986.

Arbitration Cases, Fees, and Days

Arbitration Cases Decided

As already observed, in addition to judging grievance and interest disputes, arbitrators often work as mediators or fact-finders and also serve in other neutral capacities. However, only grievance and interest arbitration cases are relevant to the present analysis.

Grievance Cases. Table 6.1 shows that labor arbitrators in the United States decided an average of 24 grievances apiece during 1986. NAA members averaged 56 grievance decisions (henceforth, cases), three-and-one-half times more than the typical non-NAA arbitrator's caseload. Much of this difference is due partly to the relatively high proportion of NAA members who were full-time arbitrators (43%) as opposed to non-NAA

Table 6.2
Interest Cases (1986)

Variables	non-NAA	NAA	Total
Interest	1.21	1.79	1.33
Decisions	(193)	(336)	(529)
w/o zero[1]	3.82	4.31	3.95
	(61)	(140)	(201)
Work Status***, w/o zero***			
Full-time	3.87	2.18	3.37
	(30)	(146)	(176)
w/o zero	6.82	4.90	6.01
	(17)	(81)	(98)
Part-time	0.72	1.08	0.77
	(163)	(190)	(353)
w/o zero	2.66	3.49	2.80
	(44)	(59)	(103)

[1] Second mean computed on the basis of arbitrators who decided at least one interest case in 1986.

*** Difference is statistically significant at $\alpha = .001$ (two-tailed tests).

members (16%).[1] In 1986 full-time arbitrators decided more than four times as many cases as part-timers. Table 6.1 also shows that full-time NAA arbitrators handed down nearly 69 percent more grievance decisions than full-time arbitrators who were not part of the Academy, and that part-time NAA arbitrators decided more than three times as many cases as their nonmember counterparts.

Grievance arbitration earnings derive from the number of grievance cases decided, and the latter vary directly with work status and NAA/non-NAA membership status. Thus, these factors should also affect earnings differences.

Interest Cases. The average number of interest cases decided in 1986 was much smaller than the corresponding number of grievance awards handed down (Table 6.2). Sixty-two percent of active arbitrators did not judge a single interest case. The average number of interest decisions issued by those who had cases was approximately four.

The distribution of interest arbitration cases decided in 1986 generally follows the same patterns as grievance awards described in Table 6.2.

Table 6.3
1986 Grievance Cases: Per Diem Fee

Variables	non-NAA	NAA	Total
Per Diem Fee***	$374.89 (188)	$435.95 (330)	$387.89 (518)
Work Status**			
Full-time***	$375.93 (27)	$452.04 (141)	$409.87 (168)
Part-time***	$374.72 (161)	$423.94 (189)	$382.26 (350)

** Difference is statistically significant at $a = .01$; *** at $a = .001$ (two-tailed tests).

NAA members decided more interest cases than nonmembers, but the difference is quite small and it is not statistically significant.

When work status and NAA membership are both considered, full-time, non-NAA arbitrators decided significantly more interest cases than their NAA colleagues, but the reverse holds true with part-time arbitrators. These findings suggest that new arbitrators in relatively larger numbers may be entering the profession through the public sector's interest case route. Nevertheless, for most arbitrators, the earnings generated from interest as compared to grievance cases is quite small.

Arbitration Fees

Labor arbitrators charge a variety of fees for their services. Virtually all arbitrators in the United States set a per diem fee for time spent (1) traveling to and from hearings, (2) hearing cases, (3) conducting executive sessions, and (4) studying and drafting awards. Moreover, most arbitrators impose a case cancellation fee; some assess a docketing fee; and a few have other administrative or miscellaneous fixed assessments. All of these fee and charge categories are component elements of grievance and interest arbitration earnings.

Grievances: Per Diem Fee. Table 6.3 shows that the average per diem charge for grievances in 1986 was $388: a mean that varies from $436 for NAA members to $375 for the typical nonmember. The NAA and non-NAA per diem fee difference continues to hold after controlling for work status differences. Further, *within* the membership status category, full-time arbitrators averaged higher fees than part-time arbitrators. Some of

Table 6.4
1986 Grievance Cases: Cancellation Fee

Variables	non-NAA	NAA	Total
Cancellation Fee***	$180.86 (187)	$347.74 (322)	$215.86 (509)
w/o zero***	$264.23 (128)	$380.86 (294)	$294.72 (422)
Work Status*, w/o zero***			
Full-time**	$283.81 (27)	$386.58 (138)	$329.09 (165)
w/o zero*	$348.32 (22)	$401.11 (133)	$373.78 (155)
Part-time***	$163.49 (160)	$318.61 (184)	$186.84 (344)
w/o zero***	$246.77 (106)	$364.13 (161)	$269.03 (267)

* Difference is statistically significant at $a = .05$; ** at $a = .01$; *** at $a = .001$ (two-tailed tests).

the difference in annual earnings between NAA and non-NAA arbitrators is tied to differences in per diem grievance fees.

Grievances: Cancellation Fee. Table 6.4 shows that the average 1986 cancellation fee in grievance cases was $216, ranging from zero to $650. Most labor arbitrators charge a cancellation fee. About ninety percent of NAA arbitrators and seventy percent of non-NAA arbitrators had cancellation fee policies. For those who did, the overall mean was $295.

Among arbitrators charging cancellation fees, NAA members and full-time arbitrators charged more than their respective counterpart classifications. These differences were expected inasmuch as the opportunity costs for reserving a (canceled) hearing day are higher for busier arbitrators.

Grievances: Docketing and Miscellaneous Fee. Less than 10 percent of arbitrators charged docketing fees in 1986. For this reason, tabulations are not presented. The mean reported docketing fee was $69. The docketing fee for NAA and non-NAA members, respectively, were $82 and $64; and full-time arbitrators who charged for docketing assessed fees for $78, while part-timers charged $68.

The miscellaneous fees category is a residual, catch-all category. In 1986 about 10 percent of U.S. arbitrators routinely charged for services not already covered by the per diem, cancellation, and docketing fee categories. This fee was largely assessed for "postponements" and "overhead expense recovery." NAA members and nonmembers alike averaged about $263 in miscellaneous fees.

Because such a small proportion of arbitrators charged docketing and miscellaneous fees, these categories should not add significantly to understanding the underlying forces which account for 1986 average annual earnings from arbitration.

Interest: Per Diem Fee. As previously observed, a little more than one-third of all active arbitrators decided interest cases in 1986. Among those who did, the average number of interest cases decided was dwarfed by grievance cases. These facts suggest that the share of arbitration earnings originating in interest work should be quite small, unless, of course, the lack of interest—relative to grievance—cases was offset by large positive differences in per diem (and other) interest fees and/or in the number of days spent per interest case.

These differences, however, did not exist. Only a few dollars separate the per diem, cancellation, docketing, and other fees that arbitrators charged for interest cases as opposed to grievance cases: arbitrators usually charge more for interest cases, but not much more. This finding held up even when NAA membership and work status were considered (compare the means in Tables 6.3 and 6.4 against those in Tables 6.5 and 6.6, respectively). The NAA study did not differentiate between days spent per interest case versus per grievance case. Thus, it is impossible to say whether a difference in days spent per case would have had a significant effect on the share of total arbitration earnings resulting from interest work.

Arbitration Days

Arbitration earnings are also related to the number of days spent on each case—the days allocated to (1) hearings, (2) cancellations/postponements, (3) study and drafting, (4) travel, and (5) executive sessions in both grievance and interest cases. This information is reported in Tables 6.7 through 6.11. These tabulations refer to *mean days per year (1986)* and not to *mean days per case*.

Hearing Days. In 1986, the typical arbitrator billed the parties for 19 hearing days (see Table 6.7). The respective means for NAA members and nonmembers were 45 and 14 days. Proportionately speaking, this mean difference corresponds to the mean difference reported for cases decided. Similarly, average hearing days cross-tabulated by NAA/non-NAA membership status and work status conform to the pattern of means of cases decided (see Table 6.1).[2]

Cancellation and Postponement Days. Table 6.8 suggests that the num-

Table 6.5
1986 Interest Cases: Per Diem Fee

Variables	non-NAA	NAA	Total
Per Diem Fee***	$365.00	$472.61	$393.56
	(58)	(136)	(194)
w/o zero***	$365.00	$476.11	$394.33
	(45)	(135)	(193)
Work Status*, w/o zero*			
Full-time***	$375.00	$510.71	$437.69
	(14)	(78)	(92)
w/o zero***	$375.00	$510.71	$437.69
	(14)	(78)	(92)
Part-time	$361.82	$421.38	$371.87
	(44)	(58)	(102)
w/o zero*	$361.82	$428.77	$372.96
	(44)	(57)	(101)

* Difference is statistically significant at $\alpha = .05$; *** at $\alpha = .001$ (two-tailed tests).

ber of cancellation and postponement days reported are also related to the number of grievances decided. The average number of billed cancellation and postponement days in 1986 was nearly 3.4. Because the typical arbitrator decides about 24 cases (Table 6.1), roughly speaking, arbitrators charged a cancellation fee in one out of eight cases decided.

Study and Drafting Days. Adding to the earnings story, Table 6.9 shows that an average of 26 days was spent studying and drafting arbitration decisions in 1986. Of significance, however, are the sizable within-classification differences in study and drafting days shown in this table. Thus, the studying and drafting aspect of days worked should affect earnings differences in a major way.

The average NAA arbitrators allocated four times more days per year to studying and drafting than non-NAA arbitrators—70 to 17. This was expected because NAA members conducted more hearings. However, the typical NAA arbitrator spent only about three times more hearing days than non-NAA arbitrators (Table 6.7). Comparing mean values from

Table 6.6
1986 Interest Cases: Cancellation Fee

Variables	non-NAA	NAA	Total
Cancel./Post. Fee[***]	$145.43 (58)	$315.05 (134)	$263.80 (192)
w/o zero[***]	$290.86 (29)	$390.88 (108)	$327.33 (137)
Work Status[***], w/o zero[***]			
Full-time	$275.00 (14)	$334.08 (76)	$324.89 (90)
w/o zero	$385.00 (10)	$409.52 (62)	$396.98 (72)
Part-time[***]	$104.20 (44)	$290.09 (58)	$209.90 (102)
w/o zero[***]	$241.32 (19)	$365.76 (46)	$275.13 (65)

[***] Difference is statistically significant at $\alpha = .001$ (two-tailed tests).

Table 6.7
Hearing Days (1986)

Variables	non-NAA	NAA	Total
Hearing Days[***]	13.89 (165)	44.63 (226)	19.25 (391)
Work Status[***]			
Full-time	45.15 (20)	68.53 (80)	54.06 (100)
Part-time[***]	5.58 (145)	31.53 (146)	12.53 (291)

[***] Difference is statistically significant at $\alpha = .001$ (two-tailed tests).

Table 6.8
Cancelled/Postponed Days (1986)

Variables	non-NAA	NAA	Total
Cancelled/ Postponed Days***	1.69 (166)	11.34 (231)	3.40 (397)
Work Status***			
Full-time***	4.50 (20)	17.98 (84)	9.80 (104)
Part-time***	1.31 (146)	7.54 (147)	2.15 (293)

*** Difference is statistically significant at α = .001 (two-tailed tests).

Table 6.9
Study and Drafting Days (1986)

Variables	non-NAA	NAA	Total
Study and Drafting Days***	16.55 (165)	70.06 (226)	25.88 (391)
Work Status***			
Full-time***	43.60 (20)	105.28 (80)	67.12 (100)
Part-time***	12.82 (145)	50.77 (146)	17.92 (291)

*** Difference is statistically significant at α = .001 (two-tailed tests).

Tables 6.7 and 6.9 in this way suggests that Academy members spent about 1.6 study/drafting days per hearing day compared to 1.2 study/drafting days per hearing day for nonmembers. Directly computing the mean number of study/drafting days spent per hearing day (per case), the 1986 estimate for NAA and non-NAA members is 1.45 and 1.1, respectively. These ratios are smaller than the conventionally stated ratio of two study/drafting days per day of hearing.

Travel Days. Throughout calendar year 1986 labor arbitrators charged for an average of 2.5 days of travel (see Table 6.10). Apparently, the parties tend to minimize arbitration costs by selecting arbitrators who are

Table 6.10
Travel Days (1986)

Variables	non-NAA	NAA	Total
Travel Days***	1.41	7.70	2.52
	(123)	(231)	(396)
Work Status***			
Full-time***	3.00	10.59	5.96
	(20)	(83)	(103)
Part-time***	1.19	6.07	1.85
	(145)	(148)	(293)

*** Difference is statistically significant at α = .001 (two-tailed tests).

Table 6.11
Executive Session Days (1986)

Variables	non-NAA	NAA	Total
Executive Session Days***	.21	.99	.35
	(165)	(229)	(394)
Work Status***			
Full-time	.70	1.45	.99
	(20)	(80)	(100)
Part-time**	.14	.74	.23
	(145)	(149)	(294)

** Difference is statistically significant at α = .01; *** at α = .001 (two-tailed tasts).

within easy commuting distances of hearing venues. Not shown in Table 6.10 is the estimate that arbitrators spent one day travelling for every five cases decided. For NAA and non-NAA members, respectively, the comparable day of travel per case ratio is 1:3 and 1:6.

Table 6.10 also shows that NAA members and full-time arbitrators billed for more travel days than did nonmember and part-timers. This is to be expected because the busier one is, the greater is the likelihood of travel.[3]

Executive Session Days. Differences in annual earnings are not likely to vary to a significant degree because of differences in days billed by arbitrators for presiding over post-hearing executive sessions. Averages for days spent in executive session are shown in Table 6.11. The typical arbitrator billed for less than one executive session day in 1986.

Table 6.12
Reported Earnings per Case (1986)

Variables	non-NAA	NAA	Total
Earnings per Case**	$1072.4 (182)	$1238.8 (305)	$1106.5 (487)
Gender			
Male**	$1085.4 (162)	$1245.5 (294)	$1120.4 (456)
Female	$967.0 (20)	$1059.1 (11)	$974.2 (31)
Work Status			
Full-time***	$922.5 (26)	$1261.9 (125)	$1066.9 (151)
Part-time	$1097.4 (156)	$1222.8 (180)	$1116.3 (336)

** Difference is statistically significant at $a = .01$; *** at $a = .001$ (two-tailed tests).

Arbitration Earnings

Two measures of arbitration earnings were constructed from information provided by the Academy's sample of labor arbitrators who issued at least one decision during 1986. The first measure, referred to as "reported earnings," is based on the survey question: "Excluding expenses, what was the average amount billed for a case in 1986?" The arbitrator's answer to this question was multiplied by the number of grievance and interest decisions handed down in 1986. This product constitutes reported earnings, which are analyzed in Table 6.13.

The second measure is referred to as "computed grievance earnings." This measure is the product of each arbitrator's 1986 grievance cases multiplied by days (by type) spent per case and fees (by type) per day, added to 1986 grievance earnings from cancellations, postponements, docketing, and miscellaneous sources.[4]

Reported Earnings

Nearly all active arbitrators in the study reported their 1986 average earnings per (grievance and interest) case net of expenses. Table 6.12

shows that average 1986 net earnings per case was $1,106, with significantly different means of $1,239 and $1,072 for Academy and non-Academy members, respectively. The NAA/non-NAA earnings per case difference remains even after the data are cross-classified by gender and work status. However, only the differences in NAA/non-NAA earnings per case among male and full-time arbitrators are statistically significant.

It is interesting to observe that NAA and non-NAA males reported larger per case earnings than their female counterparts. Yet, Table 6.13 shows that in 1986, women earned more than men: $26,580 and $67,070 for non-NAA and NAA females versus $14,100 and $64,607 for their respective male opposites. All of these mean differences miss statistical significance. Nevertheless, the next part of this chapter will account for them in terms of inter-gender differences in per diem fees, billed days, and cases decided.

To some, labor arbitration is not a particularly affluent profession. Its overall average income was only $25,574 in 1986 (see Table 6.13). By comparison, the overall average income for professional employees and lawyers was $31,616 and $39,520 in 1986, respectively.[5] However, a more credible comparison figure is probably $67,629, the 1986 mean earnings of full-time arbitrators.

Reported earnings for NAA members in 1986 were $64,696. This was more than four times the earnings of non-Academy members. Full-time NAA members averaged $98,850 from their practices in 1986, more than twice as much as that earned by full-time nonmembers. However, the vast majority of the arbitration profession's practitioners work part-time, and their earnings, whether in the Academy or not, decline accordingly. The typical part-timer earned only about $15,000 in 1986, as reported in Table 6.13.

Clearly, earnings from labor arbitration are anything but uniform. Figure 6.1 shows that the profession's $25,574 mean was drawn from a highly skewed distribution of earnings. Less than 5 percent of active arbitrators earned $100,000 or more in 1986, while 46 percent earned $10,000 or less. More than three-fourths of active, U.S. arbitrators earned $30,000 or less from their practices in 1986.

Table 6.13 strongly suggests that membership in the National Academy of Arbitrators and work status are significant and positive correlates with reported 1986 earnings.[6] Further, Figure 6.2 adds the suggestion that accumulated professional experience (i.e., career caseload) may also be an independent determinant of current earnings.

To expand on the latter point, the top diagram in Figure 6.2 shows the overall relationship between reported earnings and career caseload (without controlling for membership status), whereas, the bottom diagram in Figure 6.2 shows the relationship among reported earnings, career caseload, and membership status. Both diagrams demonstrate that current

Table 6.13
Reported Earnings[1] (1986)

Variables	non-NAA	NAA	Total
Cases Decided***	16.22	52.84	23.74
	(182)	(305)	(487)
Reported Earnings***	$15,471	$64,696	$25,574
Gender			
Male Cases***	14.65	52.47	22.91
	(162)	(294)	(456)
Rep. Earn.***	$14,100	$64,607	$25,138
Female Cases	28.95	63.00	31.61
	(20)	(11)	(31)
Rep. Earn.	$26,580	$67,070	$29,744
Work Status (Cases* Rep. Earn.***)**			
Full-time Cases**	49.39	52.47	61.86
	(26)	(125)	(151)
Rep. Earn.***	$44,499	$98,850	$67,629
Part-time Cases***	10.69	34.90	14.35
	(156)	(180)	(336)
Rep. Earn.***	$10,634	$40,978	$15,214

[1] This computation does not equal the product of average number of cases times average reported earnings. Reported earnings is the summed product of cases per arbitrator multiplied by reported average earnings per arbitrator divided by all arbitrators.

** Difference is statistically significant at $\alpha = .01$; *** at $\alpha = .001$ (two-tailed tests).

earnings steadily increase with lifetime caseload. This prompts the observation that accumulated experience may also be a determinant of arbitration earnings.

The top panel in Figure 6.2 shows that the typical arbitrator who decided

Figure 6.1
Distribution of Reported Earnings (1986)

Arbitrators

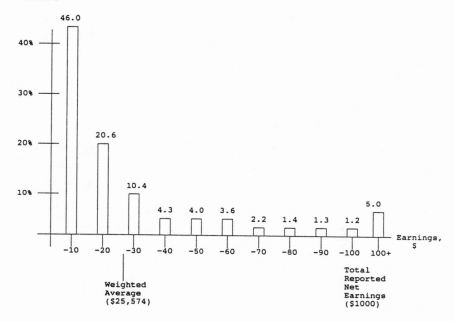

fewer than 500 cases during a career lifetime, averaged about $15,000 in arbitration earnings in 1986. In contrast, the arbitrator who decided between 500 and 999 lifetime cases earned slightly more than $54,000, representing an almost fourfold increment in earnings, or nearly $40,000. The absolute magnitude of this increment is much larger than any other found in Figure 6.2. If this step-up in earnings defines "economic viability" from the practice of arbitration, then accumulating about 500 decisions as quickly as possible would seem to be an important pursuit for aspiring arbitrators.

The foregoing analysis makes it clear that deciding to become a full-time career arbitrator entails economic sacrifices and risks. First, over the course of a career, arbitration earnings may not be as high as the earning streams available from kindred pursuits requiring similar backgrounds and preparations. Second, making it to the right-hand tail of the arbitration earnings distribution (see Figure 6.1) may be too iffy a proposition to risk. These two considerations may account for the fact that in 1986 less than one-half of the labor arbitrators in this sample practiced on a full-time basis; and further, that most arbitrators' economic livelihood is largely dependent on earnings from non-arbitration pursuits.

Figure 6.2
Reported Earnings by Career Caseload (1986)

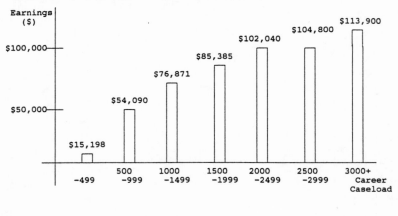

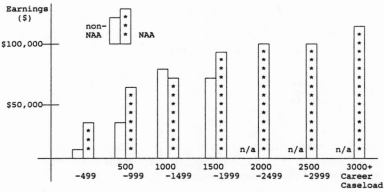

	-499	500 -999	1000 -1499	1500 -1999	2000 -2499	2500 -2999	3000+
non-NAA	$13,029	$35,010	$82,400	$76,250	N/A	N/A	N/A
NAA	$38,250	$61,640	$74,949	$93,290	$102,040	$104,080	$113,900

A Detour into Gender Differences

The gender-based means reported in Tables 6.12 and 6.13 derive from 1987 samples of 456 male and 31 female arbitrators who decided at least one case in 1986. How credible are the female arbitrator estimates? A sample of 31 active female arbitrators seems too small!

Perhaps the best way to answer this question is to begin by pointing out that in 1987 there were only about 279 women arbitrators in the whole country, 27 NAA members and 252 nonmembers. (Refer to Table 1.4 in Chapter 1.) About 20 percent of both populations were inactive in 1986. Thus, the sample of twenty non-NAA women represented about 10 percent of all active nonmember women arbitrators, and the eleven NAA female members represented approximately 50 percent of the 1987 population of active women Academy members. Yes, these samples of women arbitrators are small, but so too are the populations from whence they came. Furthermore, the ratios of male and female arbitrators—NAA and non-NAA—present in the samples mirror the underlying ratios present in the populations of arbitrators. Finally, however, it is partly because of the small female samples that their reported earnings per case (Table 6.12) and reported earnings (Table 6.13) were not significantly different from the comparable male estimates at conventional levels of statistical significance.

Turning to the gender means in Table 6.14, NAA members, both men and women, decided more cases than non-NAA members. This story is largely repeated for the other variable means appearing in this table: grievance per diem fees, hearing days, and study and drafting days. Again, partly due to sample size, none of the mean differences involving women are statistically significant.

Nevertheless, Table 6.14 documents the point that was hinted at earlier, namely, in 1986 women arbitrators tended to hand down more grievance cases (31) than men (24), a pattern which holds even after controlling for NAA/non-NAA membership status. This difference explains how men could average more earnings per case (Table 6.12), while women averaged higher annual reported earnings (Table 6.13).

Why did men outdo women when it came to 1986 earnings per case? Table 6.14 sheds light on this question. It appears that male arbitrators charged more per day and may have billed for more days per case than female arbitrators. Table 6.15 reports that male arbitrators averaged about 3 days per grievance case, compared to female arbitrators' average of 2.5 days per case.

Computed Grievance Earnings

Arbitration earnings are dominated by grievance earnings. Thus, by identifying the sources of grievance arbitration earnings, a giant step is taken toward understanding both earnings differences and the makeup of total earnings.

Table 6.15 depicts computed grievance earnings. These estimates differ from reported earnings in both definition and sample. The means in Table 6.13 are based on 487 observations, while those in Table 6.15 are based on 385 observations. The data required to construct the computed griev-

Table 6.14
Grievance Cases, Grievance Per Diem Fees, Hearing Days, and Study and Drafting Days by Gender (1986)

Variables	non-NAA	NAA	Total
Male*			
Grievance Cases	14.7	55.2	23.7
	(173)	(324)	(497)
Grievance Per Diem Fees	$376.9	$436.6	$390.4
	(168)	(319)	(487)
Hearing Days	12.4	45.1	18.5
	(150)	(221)	(371)
Study and Drafting Days	16.4	70.9	26.5
	(150)	(221)	(371)
Female			
Grievance Cases	27.4	69.1	30.9
	(20)	(12)	(32)
Grievance Per Diem* Fees	$358.5	$418.2	$363.2
	(20)	(11)	(31)
Hearing Days	28.3	23.2	28.1
	(15)	(5)	(20)
Study and Drafting Days	18.3	32.4	19.0
	(15)	(5)	(20)

* Difference is statistically significant at $\alpha = .01$ (two-tailed tests).

ance earnings were such that about 100 responses were deleted from this analysis because they lacked information on some requisite variable(s). Thus, for reasons of definition and sample, the earnings estimates appearing in Tables 6.13 and 6.15 should differ.

One sees toward the bottom of the "NAA-Membership" column in Table 6.15 that non-NAA members earned about 21 percent of member earnings in 1986: $12,715 versus $60,652. Moreover, it can be seen that this differential stems from the fact that non-NAA members versus NAA members decided about one-third as many cases and earned about one-third less per case decided. Nonmember earnings per case lagged behind NAA member earnings per case because the former averaged fewer days per case, lower fees per day, and levied lower per case charges for cancellations, docketing, and so forth.

Table 6.15
Computed Grievance Earnings (1986)

Variables	NAA-Membership Non-NAA NAA	Gender Female Male	Work Status Part-Time Full-Time	Total (385)[1]
Number of Cases	13.99*** 42.67	27.35 18.28	12.24*** 53.77	19.01
Number of Days of HD,ST,TR,ES per Case	2.84** 3.56	2.51 3.00	3.01 2.73	2.96
Per Diem Fee	$374.50*** $430.98	$360.78 $386.44	$380.48 $404.42	$384.38
Cancellation Fee per Case	$36.98*** $115.20	$52.97 $50.46	$45.97** $74.75	$50.66
Docketing Fee per Case	$5.53 $11.11	$0.59** $7.02	$7.17 $3.08	$6.50
Miscellaneous Fee per Case	$25.60 $27.85	$5.49*** $27.79	$24.36 $34.41	$25.99
Computed Earnings Grievance Case	$1,138** $1,674	$997 $1,253	$1,235 $1,219	$1,232
Computed Earnings from Grievance Arbitration	$12,715*** $60,652	$19,746 $21,223	$13,709*** $59,060	$21,104
Number of Observations	162 223	20 365	287 96	385

[1] Number of arbitrators who had at least one grievance case in 1986.

** Difference is statistically significant at $a = .01$; *** at $a = .001$ (two-tailed tests).

Computed grievance arbitration earnings for female and male arbitrators averaged $19,746 and $21,223, respectively, as indicated near the bottom of the "Gender" column in Table 6.15. This difference is not statistically significant. Females decided 49 percent more grievance arbitration cases than males, whereas males earned more per case than females. On average, men spent more days per case and charged slightly higher per diem fees than did females. These findings are consistent with the results discussed earlier relative to reported earnings.

Grievance arbitration earnings for full and part-time arbitrators averaged $59,060 and $13,709, respectively, in 1986. This difference in earnings is almost entirely attributable to the difference in the number of cases decided by each group. The difference in computed earnings per case between full and part-time grievance arbitrators is not significant.

Summation and Conclusions

Arbitration earnings for 1986 was the focus of this chapter. Arbitrators who failed to decide a single case in 1986 were omitted from this analysis. Thus, it can readily be argued that the earnings estimates presented herein are *biased upward*. This view is supported by the fact that some inactive arbitrators were in the beginning phase of their careers. Like new lawyers or doctors waiting for business, these individuals were *no less* arbitrators merely because they were waiting for the market to discover their availability. Moreover, other inactive arbitrators were temporarily unavailable because of illness or injury. Nevertheless, they too are arbitrators. For these reasons, these responding arbitrators arguably should have been included in this chapter's analysis. Their exclusion produces the concern about biased results.

A different view is that arbitrators who are not used are arbitrators in name only. After all, according to this argument, there is no official directory or registry of arbitrators in the United States. Anyone can be labelled an arbitrator. From this perspective, the above-noted groups of arbitrators were rightly dropped from the analysis, and the reported earnings are *unbiased*. Without attempting to resolve this debate, this chapter merely advises readers to limit their generalization of its earnings estimates to arbitrators who decided at least one case in 1986.

Clearly, arbitration earnings are the product of cases decided, days spent per case, and fees charged per day. Membership in the NAA is positively related to all three of these factors, but *mainly* to cases decided. Explaining why NAA members decide so many more cases than non-NAA members is a subject for separate analysis. However, this chapter's findings suggest that NAA membership may signal information to the parties about differences in arbitrator "quality" that otherwise would be costly for them to acquire.

Other considerations held constant, the parties may screen arbitrators on criteria like "the highest standards of integrity, competence, honor, . . . character . . . acceptance of and adherence to the Code of Professional Responsibility . . . [and] the study and understanding of the arbitration of labor-management disputes . . . "[7] A history of considerable arbitration experience plus these criteria are precisely what govern admission into the Academy. Consequently, if both Academy membership selections and the parties' arbitrator choices are based on the same criteria, then choosing the typical NAA member (sight unseen) over a typical non-NAA member (sight unseen) may reduce what economists call the parties' "search costs." Without this quality signal, the parties may engage in costly background research on every arbitrator named on every listing.

Earnings from the practice of labor arbitration in the United States are lower than might be expected relative to other professions whose members have similar backgrounds and academic preparations. However, unlike law, education, medicine, and kindred professions, labor arbitration is largely a part-time pursuit. Because of this, arbitration earnings are low. (Or, is it that arbitrators practice part-time because earnings are so low?) The typical labor arbitrator in this country earns about three-fourths of total income from other lines of work.

Clearly, NAA members (some of whom work full-time) and full-time arbitrators (many of whom are NAA members) earn relatively good arbitration incomes. But to be included among these groups takes time, sometimes a lot of time. To be repeatedly chosen as an arbitrator by a number of different parties is positively related to accumulated experience. As already noted, the one variable explaining the earnings difference between NAA and non-NAA member arbitrators was cases decided. Obviously, it is this variable that also accounts for earnings difference between full-time and part-time arbitrators. One of this chapter's more pleasant discoveries is that women arbitrators earned as much as, if not more than, their male colleagues in 1986. The chapter's detour into gender comparisons prompts a few observations. Although women were not very well represented in the profession in 1987, they appear to have had little trouble securing cases. In 1986, women averaged more cases than men, a difference which caused their annual earnings to match, perhaps exceed, those of male arbitrators. The parties may be following the strategy of selecting women over men arbitrators when they get the chance, holding other differences constant.

Unfortunately, the base number of minority arbitrators practicing in the United States was so small in 1987 (refer to Chapters 1 and 2) that making interracial arbitrator comparisons is of little consequence. It is important to increase the share of practicing women arbitrators in this country, and it is equally important to attract minorities to the profession. This analysis cautiously demonstrated that women have found acceptability as arbitrators. A similar conclusion is yet to be drawn with respect to minority arbitrators.

In summation, choosing to arbitrate as a career may be risky for some. Overall mean earnings are not high relative to other professions—but to most, arbitration is a part-time activity—and the earnings distribution is highly skewed with a long right-hand tail. Making it to the upper end of the tail may take years, if it happens at all. Facing the choice of low probable "feast" or high probable "famine," it is no wonder that most labor arbitrators have alternate sources of income and/or are older, many enjoying retirement benefits from an earlier career.

Notes

1. This is not to say that NAA membership causes a higher probability of becoming a full-time arbitrator. Indeed, causation may run in the opposite direction: full-time status (acceptance) increases the probability of becoming an NAA member.

2. Table 6.1 is based on responses from 529 practicing arbitrators. Of this total, only 391 arbitrators provided information required to construct Table 6.7. Reporting lower means for "grievance and interest hearing days" than for "grievance cases decided" may be due to this sampling difference. Furthermore, many cases are heard in less than a full day.

3. This general proposition, however, does not seem to hold for NAA women versus NAA men. On average, the caseloads of NAA men demanded more travel by a margin of eight-to-one. It may be that women get relatively more state and local public sector cases.

4. A parallel calculation can also be made for earnings from interest cases. Then, by adding together computed earnings from both grievance and interest arbitrations, an alternate measure of earnings—one that would be strictly comparable to "reported earnings"—would be available. However, this was not done. To compute *both* grievance and interest earnings for *each* respondent in the NAA survey required information on a large number of variables. Thus, after dropping respondent files lacking complete information, the resulting sample size was only about 25 percent of the 487 arbitrators who were included in the analysis underlying Table 6.13's construction. Further, the missing information problem was dominant in the area of interest earnings. In any case, to limit sample size erosion, only data on "computed grievance earnings" are subsequently analyzed in Table 6.15.

5. Sources from U.S. Department of Labor, Bureau of Labor Statistics, *Labor Force Statistics Derived from the Current Population Survey, 1948–87*, August 1988.

6. The reported earnings distribution for non-NAA members is akin to that shown in Figure 6.1. As for NAA members, the earnings distribution is relatively more uniform. The reported earnings distributions for part and full-time arbitrators are sharply skewed to the right and left, respectively.

7. National Academy of Arbitrators, *The Constitution and By-Laws* (includes all Amendments through May 23, 1984), p. 3.

7

Surplus or Shortage in the Market for Arbitration Services: NAA Membership Status, Work Status, and Geographic Dimensions

*Mario F. Bognanno and
Clifford E. Smith*

Introduction

Union and employer advocates seldom mention that arbitration services or arbitrators are in plentiful supply. More often heard are complaints that "the same tired names are listed time and time again," or "arbitrators take too long to decide a case because of huge backlogs" and "scheduling delays are extreme." Anecdotes like these are heard from coast to coast. They clearly emphasize the parties' belief that shortages predominate.

But opinions do differ. Practicing arbitrators often complain about surpluses. This opinion is so self-serving that some would dismiss it outright were it not for the fact that many highly esteemed and responsible arbitrators have advanced it. For example, during his 1984 Presidential Address before the National Academy of Arbitrators, Professor Mark Kahn's answer to the question, "Is there a shortage of good arbitrators?" was as follows:

Although there are plenty of would-be arbitrators, the profession is in fact a small one. The great bulk of labor arbitration is handled, in my own estimate, by about 800 persons in the United States and Canada, of whom about 540 are members of the Academy. . . .

What we do know, however, is that the impression of a shortage derives from the overwhelming preference of the parties for the old hands. For this reason, the experienced arbitrators get all they can handle (sometimes more), and the rest spills over to those with less experience. . . .

The parties who seek an arbitrator face the dilemma of a tradeoff between experience and availability.[1]

Two years later, Professor Jack Stieber more or less agreed with Kahn's surplus thesis, albeit prospectively. In a presentation before the annual educational meeting of the National Academy of Arbitrators, he predicted a decline in the absolute number of grievance cases going to arbitration. This prediction combined with increasing numbers of arbitrators led him to conclude that "[A]t some point, this must result in a decrease in average caseloads for arbitrators."[2]

Which opinion is correct? Why do arbitrators and the parties differ on this point? This chapter initiates answers to these questions. It presents a brief exploration into the demand for and supply of arbitral services and, hence, arbitrators. Whether the market for arbitration services or arbitrators is balanced, or exhibits surpluses or shortages is the question motivating this analysis. Geography—a term used in the chapter's title—is relevant here since markets may be defined and analyzed in spatial terms. The NAA survey data are used in this exploration, and the information uncovered prompts answers to the questions raised.

Studying this market's operations will help to identify possible strategies best suited for correcting any arbitrator shortages that may exist. In Chapter 6, Bognanno concluded that some arbitrators "feast" while others have "famine." Thus, the payoff to a shortage-reduction strategy featuring arbitrator/user "development" and "enhanced arbitrator utilization" initiatives, rather than "new entrant" initiatives, may be most economical. In Chapter 3, Holley reports that approximately 25 percent of arbitrators practice full-time and many of them, as well as many part-timers, reveal a preference to hear and decide more cases. Again, a strategy to increase the flow of new entrants into the arbitrator market may not yield the social returns accompanying strategies to increase the utilization rate of existing arbitrators. Furthermore, Coleman and Zirkel showed in Chapter 2 that 9 percent of arbitrators who sought cases did not get any cases at all in 1986 (although 40 percent of these were from only three states). Interestingly, information from these three chapters suggests only market surpluses, not shortages. Even so, policies to increase the pool of arbitrators' utilization rate would increase market efficiency. The parties would not be as likely to use the "same old hands" and the tradeoff between "experience and availability" would not be as costly to the parties.

Because arbitration is a reputation-based, self-employing and part-time second profession for most arbitrators,[3] it is not clear what kind of initiatives would go into an arbitrator/user development and enhanced arbitrator utilization strategy. Moreover, it is not obvious whether any initiative can substitute for individual motivation, ethics, level of effort, and high quality productivity. These attributes should have developed and surfaced during most arbitrators' first profession. The hallmark of success is often present even before becoming an arbitrator. However, this may be getting ahead of the story.

Defining Equilibrium: Shortages and Surpluses

To come to grips with the shortage or surplus question, these concepts must be defined in measurable terms. Several measures of labor market disequilibrium are available. Two of them are briefly discussed below.[4]

Normative or "Need-Based" Measure. This measure usually requires that a panel of professional experts—or a comparable mechanism—is assembled to make a qualitative judgment about the number of practitioners *needed* to serve a defined clientele. Once this providers-to-users ratio is agreed upon, it is relatively simple to determine whether a shortage or surplus exists. Multiplying this ratio by the present (forecast) number of users determines the number of practitioners *needed*. Then, by comparing the present (forecast) number *needed* with the present (forecast) number *available*, a quantitative measure of the present (forecast) number of practitioners in short or excess supply is produced.

This measure's major drawback is that it substitutes a subjective, provider-determined "need" concept for that of economic "demand."[5] But because of its simplicity, this measure will subsequently be used as an exploratory device for analyzing inter-regional differences in arbitrators-to-union membership ratios. In this instance, the *national* arbitrators-to-union membership ratio—like a ratio handed down by a panel of arbitration experts—is used as the normative ratio to which regional ratios are compared.[6]

Quantity Supplied–Quantity Demanded Measure. This measure derives from microeconomics. Herein, if the quantity of service demanded at a given price exceeds the quantity supplied at that price, a shortage exists; if not, a surplus exists; and if the quantity demanded and supplied are equal, then the market is in equilibrium. Use of this measure technically requires estimates of the parameters in fully specified demand and supply functions. This information is not presently available. Nevertheless, quantity demanded/supplied ideas lying behind this measure are used in the next part of this chapter. Just as unemployment—above "frictional"—levels suggest labor market surpluses, so too may arbitrators' revealed preferences to do more work (presumably at the going price) than they actually did.

Squeezing Out Non-NAA Arbitrators

With reference to Tables 6.13 and 6.12, the analysis showed that NAA arbitrators decided three times more cases, earned four times more income, and charged only 15 percent more *per case* than non-NAA arbitrators. The parties' demand for arbitral services by NAA arbitrators is much greater than their demand for kindred services from non-NAA arbitrators—a market structure feature also manifest in NAA versus non-NAA earnings differences—although per case charges differ relatively little along the NAA membership dimension.[7]

Since NAA and non-NAA member charges per case differ by only 15 percent and since NAA arbitrators are generally more highly demanded, it is interesting that non-NAA members get as many cases as they do. In 1986 about 63,000 grievance decisions were handed down (also reference Chapter 5, Tables 5.4 and 5.5). Of this total, about one-half were decided by NAA members and the other half by nonmembers.[8] That the non-NAA arbitrators are *not squeezed out* of the market requires explanation.

All things being equal, including charges, it seems reasonable to expect ill patients to demand treatment from experienced and widely recognized specialists from the Mayo Clinic over the treatment that could be provided by inexperienced and little known neighborhood physicians—squeezing them out of the market. This analogy applies to arbitration. All things being equal, the parties should demand NAA members to judge their disputes to the exclusion of non-NAA members. However, they do not, for reasons that can easily be explained. First, as with Mayo physicians, NAA arbitrators may not be as readily available to hear cases as are their nonmember counterparts. To avoid long delays in scheduling, some parties are willing to accept the tradeoff Kahn described.

Second, NAA arbitrators—full and part-time—who are satisfied with their current workload may refuse selections, forcing the parties to search elsewhere for their arbitrators. In this instance, arbitrator preference and not the length of the queue is at issue.

Third, some well-established nonmembers—many on their way to Academy membership—enjoy reputations that rival those of NAA members. Thus, they too are highly demanded.

For these reasons, as well as other demographic and institutional reasons,[9] non-NAA arbitrators do decide thousands of cases annually in the United States. Thus, NAA membership is not the only criterion used by the parties to select arbitrators to resolve their disputes. Nevertheless, the parties complain—as Kahn implies, perhaps the issue is whether there is a plentiful supply of "old hands."

If NAA arbitrators uniquely embody the qualities valued most by the parties, then initiatives to develop non-NAA members and to increase the utilization of (involuntary) part-timers is unlikely to fully mitigate the parties' sense that shortages abound. On the other hand, there may be room to leverage the "availability" idea as a device to get the parties to search harder among the set of nonmembers for their arbitrators.

Table 7.1
Surplus of Arbitral Services in 1986

Member	non-NAA	NAA	Weighted Total
All Arbitrators	13.4[***] (n = 178)	5.2 (n = 295)	11.8 (n = 2448)
Full-time[*]	13.0 (n = 25)	5.4 (n = 124)	9.8 (n = 480)
Part-time[***]	13.5 (n = 153)	5.0 (n = 171)	12.3 (n = 1968)

[1] Actual 1986 cases include the sum of 1986 grievance and interest cases.

[*] NAA membership difference is statistically significant at $\alpha = 0.05$.
[***] NAA membership difference is statistically significant at $\alpha = 0.01$.

An Oversupply or Dearth of Arbitrators?

Is there a shortage of arbitrators? If not, is it possible to reconcile this perception with the facts? If there is no shortage, is there a surplus or is the market clearing? If there is a surplus, what is its level and is it distributed equally among NAA and non-NAA arbitrators, full-time and part-time arbitrators, and among regions in the United States? These questions are now addressed.

Underutilization (Quantity Supplied–Quantity Demanded)

Operationally, if the difference between preferred caseload (i.e., the quantity suppliable at prevailing prices) and actual caseload (i.e., the quantity demanded at prevailing prices) is positive, surpluses are suggested; if negative, shortages are suggested. Table 7.1 depicts a positive difference between preferences and actual grievance and interest cases decided in 1986. All of the estimated means—of additional cases arbitrators reportedly would have been willing and able to hear—in this table are statistically different from zero. These statistics support a surplus finding. However, arbitrators who said they were underused in actuality might have refused additional cases (at prevailing prices) coming their way or they might have delayed hearing them. With these possibilities in mind, a more accurate conclusion to draw is that the data support a "qualified" finding that surpluses existed.

The NAA/non-NAA differences between Table 7.1's mean estimates are all statistically significant. Regardless of work-status, NAA arbitrators were closer to being fully utilized than were their nonmember counterparts, desiring respectively five more cases than they actually decided versus thirteen more cases. Furthermore, relative to actual 1986 cases decided, full-timers were closer to equilibrium than were part-timers, but even part-time NAA members were more relatively satisfied with their caseloads than were full-time nonmembers. As a final observation, Table 7.1 also discloses that part-time non-NAA arbitrators, who constituted about 68 percent of all arbitrators, reported being underutilized.

This analysis suggests that indeed the parties probably do find it somewhat more difficult to secure the arbitral services of Academy members quickly. If the parties seek first among Academy members for arbitrators, they naturally would interpret this difficulty as evidence of shortages.

Not shown in Table 7.1 is whether *all* or *some* arbitrators were underutilized. Tables 7.2 (in relation to NAA membership status) and 7.3 (in relation to work status) clarify this point. Both of these tables present a more detailed breakdown of the number of arbitrators who preferred a reduced caseload (overutilized), the same caseload (balanced), or an increased one (underutilized).

Table 7.2 shows that 7.6 percent of all arbitrators were overutilized, completing more cases than desired in 1986; 17.8 percent were in balance; and 74.6 percent were underutilized—that is, they were not as busy as they would have liked to have been. The parties in contact with the busiest (i.e., overutilized) 25.4 percent ($= 7.6 + 17.8$) of all arbitrators certainly experienced refusals or scheduling delays—furthering their impression of shortages. Furthermore, 48.4 ($= 13.2 + 35.2$) percent of all NAA members and 19.7 ($= 6.2 + 13.5$) percent of all non-NAA arbitrators were among the set of arbitrators who were either too busy or just satisfied with their arbitration workload. Thus, the noted "refusal or scheduling delays" experiences were more likely to be associated with NAA members.

By the same token, the parties most likely had little contact with the 52 percent of all NAA members and 80 percent of all non-NAA members who were not as busy as they would have liked to have been. Why clients do not turn to these arbitrators more often is a bit of a puzzle. The problem may lie in communications. Interestingly, a majority of NAA arbitrators express a desire for more cases.

Table 7.3 tells a similar story. Approximately 42 ($= 12.1 + 29.5$) percent of full-time and 35 ($= 9.9 + 25.9$) percent of part-time arbitrators were overworked or just satisfied with their caseloads. The respective remain-

Table 7.2
Surplus and Shortage of Arbitral Service by NAA Membership

Desired Change in Caseload	non-NAA		NAA		Weighted Total[1]	
	n	%	n	%	n	%
-30 or less	2	1.1	13	4.4	44	1.8
-29 - -20	1	0.6	5	1.7	19	0.8
-19 - -10	2	1.1	9	3.1	37	1.5
-9 - -1	6	2.8	12	4.1	86	3.5
Shortages	11	6.2	39	13.2	186	7.6
Balanced	24	13.5	104	35.2	436	17.8
1 - 10	63	35.4	65	22.0	801	32.8
11 - 20	50	28.1	45	15.3	625	25.5
21 - 30	8	4.5	19	6.4	120	4.9
31 - 40	4	2.3	11	3.7	62	2.5
41 - 50	11	6.2	5	1.7	129	5.3
51 or more	7	3.9	7	2.4	89	3.6
Surpluses	143	80.3	152	51.5	1826	74.6
Total	178	100.0	295	100.0	2448	100.0

[1] Weighted averages use 11.0114 and 1.6536 to weight non-NAA and NAA observations, respectively.

ders—either full or part-time—reported being underutilized. Thus, whether available to arbitrate as a full or part-time arbitrator, in 1986 a majority of arbitrators wanted more cases. These arbitrators, whether Academy or non-Academy members, dominated the market place. It is thus not surprising that their declarations of surpluses are loud and often heard.

Tables 7.4 and 7.5 are essentially mirror images of one another. They respectively show the number of cases arbitrators reported they refused in 1986 and the number of additional cases they could have heard that year. Further, they provide a rough check on the consistency of arbitrator reports.

Approximately 80 percent of non-NAA and 52 percent of NAA arbitrators reported they were willing to hear more cases than they were actually called on to decide (reference Table 7.2). In comparison, Table

Table 7.3
Surplus and Shortage of Arbitral Services by Work Status

Range	Full-time		Part-time	
	n	%	n	%
-30 or less	9	6.0	6	1.9
-29 - -20	1	0.7	5	1.5
-19 - -10	4	2.7	7	2.2
-9 - -1	4	2.7	14	4.3
Shortages	18	12.1	32	9.9
Balanced	44	29.5	84	25.9
1 - 10	27	18.1	101	31.2
11 - 20	26	17.4	69	21.3
21 - 30	14	9.4	13	4.0
31 - 40	10	6.7	5	1.5
41 - 50	5	3.3	11	3.4
51 or more	5	3.3	9	2.8
Surpluses	87	58.4	208	64.2
Total	149	100.0	324	100.0

7.4 shows that about 55 percent of NAA and 82 percent of non-NAA arbitrators reported that they did not refuse to hear any cases in 1986. The corroborating nature of these separate tabulations suggests that the underlying arbitrator self-reports are reliable.

In this same vein, 45 percent of NAA members reportedly refused cases during 1986, whereas only 18 percent of nonmembers refused cases. Furthermore, nearly 5 percent of NAA and zero percent of non-NAA arbitrators refused more than 20 cases. Indirectly, these findings further strengthen the thesis that the market strongly demands the arbitral qualities of individuals invited to Academy membership.

Despite this difference in demand, many Academy members were underused. Table 7.5 shows that about 14 percent of NAA arbitrators were prepared to decide at least 21 more cases in 1986. The level of "acceptability" these arbitrators once possessed may have eroded over the years. Another possibility is that these NAA arbitrators were willing to put in long—eighty-hour—work weeks. Or, perhaps, these individuals mistak-

Table 7.4
Number of Cases Refused in 1986

Member	non-NAA		NAA		Weighted Total	
	n	%	n	%	n	%
Total	189	100.0	321	100.0	2612	100.0
0	154	81.5	176	54.8	1987	76.1
1 - 10	33	17.4	110	34.2	545	20.9
11 - 20	2	1.0	20	6.2	55	2.1
21 - 50	0	0.0	15	4.6	25	0.9
> 50	0	0.0	0	0.0	0	0.0

Table 7.5
Willingness to Decide Added Cases in 1986

Member	non-NAA		NAA		Weighted Total	
Average	14.10		10.62		13.39	
Range	n	%	n	%	n	%
0	18	10.8	113	39.5	385	16.7
1 - 10	67	40.1	78	27.3	867	37.5
11 - 20	55	32.9	56	19.6	698	30.2
21 - 30	10	6.0	21	7.3	145	6.3
31 - 40	6	3.6	5	1.7	74	3.2
41 - 50	8	4.8	10	3.5	105	4.5
> 50	3	1.8	3	1.0	38	1.6
Total	167	100.0	286	100.0	2312	100.0

enly slipped under the Academy's admission screen. All of this is speculative, intended only to be thought-provoking. Not surprisingly, about 16 percent of non-NAA arbitrators were ready to add 21 or more cases. These could be new entrants into the field or unsuccessful "older hands." Table 7.5 suggests that large absolute and relative numbers of arbitrators wanted to decide more cases. Most, of course, were non-Academy members.

Geographic Dimension

Table 7.6 presents 1987 regional distributions of member and nonmember arbitrators based on the location of their primary offices and the distribution by region of 1988 union membership. It also shows the ratio of arbitrators per 10,000 unionists by region. The states making up each region are presented in the Appendix at the end of this chapter. These regional designations are identical to those customarily used in geographic reports issued by the United States Bureau of the Census.

The regional distributions of NAA and non-NAA members are quite similar, with a single exception: the Pacific region's concentration of nonmembers is significantly larger than its concentration of NAA members: 18.3 percent versus 13.7 percent. Rapid industrialization in this region probably has brought new arbitrators into the field faster than their career development warrants admission to Academy membership.

About 70 percent of both Academy and non-Academy arbitrators are concentrated in four regions of the United States: Mid-Atlantic (a weighted total of 22% from three states); East North Central (20.9% from five states); Pacific (17.5% from five states); and South Atlantic (10.7% from eight states and the District of Columbia). This concentration is understandable—about 75 percent of union members are also located in these regions. Apparently the labor market is working: the regional volume of arbitrators and their unionized users are highly correlated. This point is reinforced by the remarkably little inter-regional variance in the ratios of arbitrators per 10,000 union members.

One can arbitrarily designate the U.S. ratio of two arbitrators per 10,000 union members as a *normative* or "need based" indicator of regional surpluses and shortages. Using this norm, five of the nine regions in Table 7.6 may be classified as shortage regions: Mid-Atlantic East North Central East South Central, West South Central, and Mountain. The Pacific region exhibits relative equilibrium, and the remaining three regions—New England, West North Central, and South Atlantic—are more or less surplus areas.

Relative to a norm of two, the arbitrator shortage in the West South Central region—Arkansas, Louisiana, Oklahoma, and Texas—is the nation's most serious. This region *needs* about thirty more arbitrators. More-

Table 7.6
Office Location and Union Membership by Region

	non-NAA	NAA	Weighted Total	Union Membership[1] (1,000)	Ratio of Arbitrators per 10,000 Union Members
	n (%)	n (%)	n (%)	n (%)	
U.S.	262 (100.0)	358 (100.0)	3477 (100.0)	17,495 (100.0)	2.0
New Eng	19 (7.3)	19 (5.3)	241 (6.9)	1,105 (6.3)	2.2
Mid-Atl	58 (22.1)	77 (21.5)	766 (22.0)	4,271 (24.4)	1.8
E.N.Cent	54 (20.6)	80 (22.3)	727 (20.9)	4,040 (23.1)	1.8
W.N.Cent	23 (8.8)	25 (7.0)	295 (8.5)	1,236 (7.1)	2.4
S.Atl	27 (10.3)	46 (12.8)	373 (10.7)	1,677 (9.6)	2.2
E.S.Cent	10 (3.8)	15 (4.2)	135 (3.9)	768 (4.4)	1.8
W.S.Cent	8 (3.1)	22 (6.1)	124 (3.6)	757 (4.3)	1.6
Mountain	8 (3.1)	8 (2.2)	101 (2.9)	562 (3.2)	1.8
Pacific	48 (18.3)	49 (13.7)	610 (17.5)	3,079 (17.6)	2.0

[1] U.S. Department of Commerce, Bureau of the Census, Statistical Abstract of the U.S., 1990, 110th Edition; and Michael Curme, Barry Hirsh and David Macpherson, "Union Membership and Contract Coverage in the U.S., 1983-1988," Industrial and Labor Relations Review 44, no. 1 (1990), pp. 22-26.

over, the nation's largest surplus of arbitrators is concentrated in the West North Central region—Minnesota, Iowa, Missouri, North Dakota, South Dakota, Nebraska, and Kansas—where there are about fifty *unneeded* arbitrators.[10] However, as argued earlier, pressing this particular measure

Table 7.7
Surplus of Arbitral Services by Region

	non-NAA	NAA	Weighted total
Total	13.43 (178)	5.20 (295)	11.753 (2,448)
New Eng	11.81 (16)	0.27 (15)	10.355 (200)
Mid-Atl	21.61 (31)	13.46 (59)	19.764 (439)
E. N. Cent	12.02 (42)	3.87 (68)	10.395 (575)
W. N. Cent	7.88 (16)	3.71 (24)	7.093 (216)
S. Atl	8.93 (15)	3.43 (40)	7.329 (231)
E. S. Cent	31.67 (6)	8.54 (13)	25.878 (88)
W. S. Cent	15.50 (8)	-10.91 (21)	7.895 (123)
Mountain	11.75 (4)	4.86 (7)	10.286 (56)
Pacific	10.18 (38)	5.74 (43)	9.525 (490)

of shortages and surpluses would be a mistake. For example, there is no reason to believe that a norm of two is in any sense optimal. Further, by using the United States (mean) ratio as the basis for identifying over or undersupplied regions, some regions must be above (i.e., in surplus) and others below (i.e., in shortage) the norm. Thus, one can only speculate whether the parties from the West North Central region complain less about arbitrator shortages than do the parties from the West South Central region. To support this caveat, note that arbitrators, as opposed to the parties, from both of these regions generally reported that they were underutilized. Interestingly, arbitrators from the West South Central reported more underutilization than did arbitrators from the West North Central region (see Table 7.7).

Underutilization analysis should yield more valid regional insights than the above *need-based* analysis. Thus, information akin to that presented in Tables 7.1 and 7.2 is recast in geographic terms in Table 7.7.

Table 7.7, unlike Table 7.6, shows that in every region of the country, resident arbitrators exhibited an overall willingness to decide more cases than they actually decided in 1986. This index ranged from a high of 25.9 in the East South Central region—which suspiciously was designated as an area in shortage, not surplus, according to the need-based analysis—to a low of 7.1 in the West North Central region—which need-based analysis identified as a surplus region.

Strictly interpreted, the total column in Table 7.7 implies the following: critical imbalances—surpluses—between the preferred and actual number of decisions handed down were prevalent in the East South Central and Mid-Atlantic regions of the country; serious surpluses appeared in the East North Central, New England, Mountain, and Pacific regions; and less serious were the surpluses in the West North Central, South Atlantic, and West South Central regions of the country.

Interestingly, NAA members located in the West South Central part of the United States reported that they had a surplus of 1986 cases (− 10.91). Clearly, NAA members from this part of the country—and in New England (0.27)—were overly busy or just satisfied with their caseloads. Parties from these regions having trouble retaining the services of Academy members no doubt had legitimate complaints. Only moderate surpluses of cases that could have been decided by NAA members were prevalent in the other regions, except for the Mid-Atlantic and East South Central regions. National Academy members from these two regions are probably most often heard complaining about their underuse.

Caseload Trends

Whether arbitrators' caseloads in 1986 were more, less, or the same as they were five years earlier is a question answered in Table 7.8. For all arbitrators, about one-third experienced no difference in cases decided between 1981 and 1986; about one-quarter reported an increase in the number of cases decided; and the remainder either experienced a decrease or were not arbitrating in 1981. This same pattern is characteristic of the non-NAA cohort studied; however, among NAA members it is interesting that the proportion who reported a trend of growing practices is nearly equal to the proportion reporting a trend of declining practices.

Among both NAA and non-NAA arbitrators, those with growing practices are probably the ones that the parties have difficulty retaining. Thus, the parties complain. However, concurrently there were the new arbitrators with little business and those who experienced inter-period shrinkage in their practices. These arbitrators probably are among the group of practitioners who would like to be in greater demand.

Table 7.8
Five Year Caseload Trend

	Same as 5 yr ago	Differ from 5 yr ago		Not part in 5 yr ago	Weighted Total
		More	Less		
		Number of Arbitrators			
Total	929	692	549	379	2,681
non-N	65	49	36	34	2,125
NAA	129	92	97	3	556
		Percentage of Arbitrators			
Total	34.7	25.8	20.5	14.2	100.0
non-N	33.7	25.4	18.7	17.6	100.0
NAA	38.4	27.4	28.9	0.9	100.0
		Difference by Regions(%)			
New Eng	27.8	23.0	21.7	21.4	100.0
Mid-Atl	40.4	20.1	16.7	14.9	100.0
E. N. Cent	38.2	22.9	18.7	17.4	100.0
W. N. Cent	36.1	24.3	19.4	14.4	100.0
S. Atl	31.2	27.9	27.9	8.9	100.0
E. S. Cent	29.7	42.1	26.5	0.0	100.0
W. S. Cent	23.5	42.2	16.9	17.8	100.0
Mountain	46.6	32.5	20.5	0.0	100.0
Pacific	29.4	29.1	22.6	12.6	100.0

The bottom panel of Table 7.8 presents the above-referenced trend information by region. First, the East South Central and Mountain regions exhibited low ratios of arbitrators per 10,000 unionists (Table 7.6)—occurrences partly explained by the fact that the NAA survey did not identify any new arbitrators opening practices in these regions between 1981 and 1986 (Table 7.7). The arbitrators per 10,000 unionists ratio was lowest in the West South Central region, but it would have been even lower had it not been for new arbitrators who set up businesses within the previous five years.

Second, the region with the largest share of new arbitrator practitioners and arbitrators with declining practices is New England (Table 7.8). The effect of these dynamics on the arbitral market, however, has been more or less positive. Regional underutilization—including the surplus time on the hands of arbitrators with less than five years in the region, was not much of a problem (Table 7.7). Further, if the practices of NAA members were among those that were downsized, this development apparently suited them (Table 7.7 shows an NAA surplus for this region of only .27).

Third, controlling for the proportion of arbitrators who were not practicing in 1981, one can easily recompute the proportions of arbitrators whose 1986 caseloads either increased, decreased, or remained the same relative to their 1981 levels. After taking this step (calculations not reported), it is clear that no more than one-quarter of reporting arbitrators in seven of the nine regions in Table 7.8 experienced decreases in their caseloads. Somewhat larger shares of arbitrators witnessed post–1981 business losses in the East South Central and particularly in the South Atlantic regions.

Lastly, difficult as the trend information in Table 7.8 is to interpret, it is clear that considerable numbers of relatively seasoned labor arbitrators experienced secular erosion in their caseloads. Since this statement applies to all regions, it tends to lend support to the argument that surpluses are real, assuming that the business lost was not planned. Moreover, since there are offsetting shares of arbitrators whose practices grew over the 1981–86 period, there is plenty of room for labor and management representatives to interpret this as proof of shortages.

Conclusion

Surpluses, not shortages, is probably the word that best characterized the 1986 market for arbitral services and arbitrators. About three-fourths of all arbitrators (80% non-NAA and 52% NAA, and 58% full-time and 64% part-time) reported they would have liked more cases than they actually had. Moreover, between 1981 and 1986 a significant share of seasoned (i.e., five or more years of practice) arbitrators experienced caseload erosion.

These underutilized arbitrators probably did not turn down any work that came their way. Presumably they were willing and able to accommodate the parties' scheduling needs promptly and to do so at prevailing charges per case. Nevertheless, at the same time, there most definitely were NAA members and some non-NAA members who were fully scheduled. Furthermore, some of these arbitrators even reported that they were overscheduled.

More likely than not, labor and management had to work harder to schedule cases with these busy arbitrators. Thus, because arbitrators are not homogeneous, there were shortages of some arbitrators—"acceptable" arbitrators. Scheduling refusals or delays the parties encountered with reference to these arbitrators served to fuel their inventory of anecdotes of general shortages where one did not exist.

In the midst of plenty, there were shortages. That is to say all arbitrators were not always busy, but some certainly were. This integration of the chapter's findings reconciles how the parties and practicing arbitrators can legitimately draw different conclusions about a market being over or undersupplied.

Geographically, arbitrators and employed workers are not uniformly distributed across the country's many regions. In 1987–88 there were 2.4 arbitrators per 10,000 union members in the West North Central region. Among the nine regions considered, this was the highest ratio—arguably the greatest surplus area. However, arbitrators from this region ranked ninth in terms of the average number of additional cases they were willing to hear. Thus, it would be wrong to try to make too much out of the normative or ratio results presented in this chapter. Nevertheless, it is refreshing that a strong correlation exists between the number of arbitrators and union members by region. Arbitrator supplies do seem to track arbitrator demands.

Regionally, the East South Central and South Atlantic states are among the ones in which arbitrators experienced the greatest erosion of caseloads over the 1981 to 1986 period. But generally, all of the other regions had some significant share of arbitrators who lost business during this time. Having said this, it is significant that most arbitrators in all regions reported either stable or expanding caseloads. Whether the parties match with the arbitrators whose businesses were stable or growing or the not-so-busy arbitrators during this period would help to account for their perceptions. Obviously, more is heard from dissatisfied parties or arbitrators than from the satisfied ones.

NAA members were generally more satisfied with their caseloads than were nonmembers. This result stands even though about one-third of them had smaller 1986 practices than they had in 1981. These findings are consistent with the conclusion that NAA members whose practices shrunk planned for the scale-back.

Appendix

Mid-Atlantic: New York, New Jersey, Pennsylvania

East North Central: Ohio, Indiana, Illinois, Michigan, Wisconsin

Pacific: Washington, Oregon, California, Alaska, Hawaii

West North Central: Minnesota, Iowa, Missouri, North Dakota, South Dakota, Nebraska, Kansas

New England: Maine, New Hampshire, Vermont, Massachusetts, Rhode Island, Connecticut

East South Central: Kentucky, Tennessee, Alabama, Mississippi

West South Central: Arkansas, Louisiana, Oklahoma, Texas

South Atlantic: Delaware, Maryland, Washington, D.C., Virginia, West Virginia, North Carolina, South Carolina, Georgia, Florida

Mountain: Montana, Idaho, Wyoming, Colorado, New Mexico, Arizona, Utah, Nevada

Notes

1. Mark L. Kahn, "The Presidential Address: Labor Arbitration—A Plea to the Parties," in *Arbitration 1984: Absenteeism, Recent Law, Panels, and Published Decisions*, Proceedings of the 37th Annual Meeting of the National Academy of Arbitrators, ed. Walter J. Gershenfeld (Washington: BNA Books, Inc., 1984), pp. 5–6.

2. Jack Steiber, "The Future of Grievance Arbitration," in *Arbitration 1986: Current and Expanding Roles*, Proceedings of the Thirty-Ninth Annual Meeting of the National Academy of Arbitrators, ed. Walter J. Gershenfeld (Washington: BNA Books, Inc., 1986), p. 213.

3. Ninety-eight percent of arbitrators held a different job prior to entering this profession and their first case decided was at the age of 45 years—about 15 years after finishing formal education (Krislov's Chapter 4); the arbitrators' average age was 57 years (Holley's Chapter 3); and only 25 percent worked full-time in this profession (Chapters 3 and 6).

4. Mario F. Bognanno, James R. Jeffers, and Carol Oliven, "Evidence on the Physician Shortage," in *Labor and Manpower*, ed. Richard Pegnetter (Iowa City: University of Iowa, 1974), pp. 131–153.

5. For more on this measure's limitations refer to James R. Jeffers, Mario F. Bognanno, and John C. Bartlett, "On the Demand Versus Need for Medical Services and the Concept of 'Shortage'," *American Journal of Public Health* 61, no. 1 (January 1971), pp. 46–63.

6. Another measure of market equilibrium is the *Internal Rate of Return Approach* (IRR). In general, the IRR is the discount rate at which the (net) present value of a projected stream of incomes-less-costs is equal to zero. For present purposes, it measures the economic return from entry into a given profession relative to the next-best alternative use of human resources. If the IRR from entry into a given profession—relative to the alternative—is increasing (decreasing) over time, this is evidence of shortage (surplus). However, this measure is not used here because the requisite information required for its estimation is not available.

7. Why charges per case do not diverge more is the subject of separate analysis being conducted by the author.

8. From Chapter 6, Tables 6.1 and 6.13. Average number of cases multiplied

by the number of arbitrators in the group times weight = total number of cases by any group. NAA: $55.65 \times 336 \times 1.65 = 30,852$. Non-NAA: $16.22 \times 182 \times 11.01 = 32,502$.

9. Reference Chapter 4 wherein Krislov describes the "entry and acceptability" processes at work in the market for arbitrators.

10. At one extreme, the West South Central region is short about thirty arbitrators, calculated as follows: $30 \approx [(2 - 1.6) \times 75.7]$; at the other extreme, the West North Central region has a surplus of approximately fifty arbitrators, calculated as follows: $50 \approx [(2 - 2.4) \times 123.6]$.

8

The NAA Study: Summation and Conclusions

Mario F. Bognanno and Charles J. Coleman

Introduction

The authors of this book began on an exploration of the data that emerged from the 1987 study of the profession and practice of arbitration sponsored by the National Academy of Arbitrators and the NAA Research and Education Foundation. The minimal objectives of the study were to develop a database on the demographics and the practices of arbitrators, and to establish a set of statistics that could later be used for determining the extent and nature of change. But the authors and the editors hoped to do more. They wanted to tell a hitherto unknown story about arbitrators and arbitration—to complete the first comprehensive, empirical, and generalizable study of the characteristics of labor arbitrators in the United States and their practices.

Working with the most representative collection of data that has ever been gathered on arbitrators and on the practice of arbitration, the individual authors attempted to provide answers to questions about the kinds of people who become arbitrators, their education and employment background, the differences between full-time and part-time arbitrators and between NAA members and nonmembers, the sources of cases and the nature of the issues addressed, career paths, caseloads, earnings, whether there was a shortage or surplus of arbitrators, and the shape of the future. When it came to the writing itself, none of the authors were content with a simple description of their portion of the data. They all raised analytical questions designed to produce insights into the forces that shape the profession and practice of arbitration. The goal of this chapter is to summarize the findings and to trace some of the implications.

The Principal Findings

The Sample and the Population

This study was based upon information drawn from an extensive questionnaire survey that was sent to the entire membership of the National Academy of Arbitrators and to a 20 percent random sample of all of the other arbitrators in the United States. The names of the arbitrators who were sampled were drawn from lists provided by the National Academy of Arbitrators, the Federal Mediation and Conciliation Service, the American Arbitration Association, and more than 65 other agencies and directories. The response rate for Academy arbitrators was in excess of 60 percent; for non-Academy arbitrators, 45 percent. The resultant sample consisted of 529 people who were actively engaged in the practice of labor arbitration and 91 who were classified as arbitrators but who did not work at it during 1986. The study group appears to be a fair representation of labor arbitrators in the United States.

Analysis of the responses indicated that about 3,500 people based in the United States were classified as being available to serve as labor arbitrators in 1986. For the country as a whole there were approximately two labor arbitrators for every 10,000 union members. These people were spread throughout the country, but they were concentrated in the industrialized regions where the union movement was strongest. Seventy percent of these arbitrators were based in the Mid-Atlantic, the East North Central, the Pacific, and the South Atlantic states (see the Appendix to Chapter 7 for the states in each region).

Demographics

Confirming the results of earlier studies, arbitration has been and remains a profession of elderly white men. In 1987, the typical arbitrator was in the late fifties and had more than twenty years of arbitration experience. Nine out of ten were men and 97 percent were white. The men tend to be older than the women, with many more years of experience, and with considerably more cases decided in their careers.

But differences in gender seem to be tied into differences in the nature of the caseload. Surprisingly, on the average, in 1986 women did at least as well as men in terms of the number of cases they heard. But the mainstream elderly white males tended to draw the bulk of their cases from the private sector, while the younger, less experienced women were more active in the public sector. This suggests that the private sector is the home of the well-established, "mainline" arbitrator, and that the public sector may be a point of entry into the field for women and, perhaps, for many of the newer arbitrators.

As a group, arbitrators are highly educated. Although there was no single educational path that led into arbitration, virtually all of the respondents had graduated from college and a substantial majority had advanced degrees. Over half were attorneys and about one-third had a doctorate. However, for the most part there were few statistically significant relationships between the level and kind of education possessed by the arbitrator and such practice variables as caseload or earnings.

Associations. But there were consistent relationships between the arbitrator's level of activity in professional associations and caseloads. Arbitrators are usually very active in professional associations related to the fields of labor law, labor relations, and dispute resolution. The larger their arbitration practices, the higher was their rate of participation in these professional societies. The arbitrators with the highest caseloads had the highest rate of membership in organizations such as the Industrial Relations Research Association, the Society of Professionals in Dispute Resolution, the Labor Law section of the regional bar, and similar organizations. Nearly all of the busy arbitrators were listed on the panels of the American Arbitration Association, the Federal Mediation and Conciliation Service, and/or state labor relations agencies.

The National Academy of Arbitrators

Almost all of the major arbitrators in North America belong to the National Academy of Arbitrators, as do most of the leading arbitration scholars. Like the rest of the sample, NAA members tend to be married, white men, highly educated and actively involved in the professional societies of the field. They tend to be older than non-Academy arbitrators, and the average age has increased as time has passed.

Among both full and part-time arbitrators, Academy members had the largest practices and made the most money from arbitration. They were listed on more panels and drew a much larger proportion of their cases from direct selection, permanent panels, and permanent umpireships than did non-Academy arbitrators. They received significantly more of their cases from the private sector, charged a higher per diem fee, conducted more hearings, and spent considerably more time in study, travel, and executive sessions.

Most beginning arbitrators look upon the NAA as being "hallowed ground." They want to belong, often very badly. These numbers indicate that Academy membership is, in fact, something to be desired. The people who take on leadership responsibilities within the profession of arbitration invariably belong to the NAA.

The Arbitration Career

The arbitration career may be conceived as having three principal phases. The first phase, consisting of the time spent in preparation for entry, is concerned with laying the foundation for an arbitration career. The typical arbitrator finishes an extensive educational process around age thirty and works at another occupation for some years before entering the field. The largest number of arbitrators have come into this profession from advocacy or university teaching, a substantial number from the IR/HR function or work with a government agency, and some from the labor movement.

Entering the Field. People often hear the story about the youngster who follows the country doctor around and, as a result of the experience, chooses at a very early age to become a physician. This is *not* the way people choose to become arbitrators. The decision to enter this profession is a complex, sophisticated one, made much later in life, and it almost always represents a secondary or tertiary career choice.

For a few, the decision may result from a single dramatic event. One of the respondents to the NAA study, for example, indicated that he was brought into arbitration as a result of witnessing the "Memorial Day Massacre."[1] But the data suggest that for most people, the decision to become an arbitrator is rooted in some prior decision that leads an individual into some other part of the labor relations field.

A person may decide to study law, and in so doing become fascinated by labor law, and become a labor attorney; to take on graduate study in economics, history, or industrial relations, develop an interest in collective bargaining and become an advocate; or, as a result of an undergraduate course in management, decide to seek a job in IR/HR or to go to work for the NLRB or a state labor relations agency. Then, after becoming a labor lawyer, an advocate, or a specialist in industrial relations, the person develops an interest in arbitration as a career. With some people, the decision is made relatively quickly, while others wait until they retire from their primary occupation to become arbitrators.

Although the data have shown that these kinds of career choices precede entry into arbitration, still unknown is what triggers the decision to make the career change and enter this field. Although the NAA study has provided a framework for understanding the choice to enter arbitration, further research is necessary to understand the complex dynamics that bring people into this profession.

Breaking In. How do arbitrators get their first cases? Two factors appear to be important. The first is visibility. As mentioned previously, the NAA data showed consistent positive relationships between membership in professional societies and caseload. The people who choose arbitrators have a limited supply of information about prospective new entrants. They probably tend to select an arbitrator they know over one they do not. Thus, they may pick the person they met who was an intern of a well-known arbitrator or whose presentation they heard at an IRRA meeting, or whose article they read. Getting selected for cases seems to be affected by visibility-enhancing activities like these.

The second factor comes out of scarcity in parts of the labor market for arbitrators. Although there probably is no scarcity of arbitrators *per se*, it invariably takes longer to find compatible dates with a mainline arbitrator than it does with a new one. Rather than to wait three months for established arbitrator X, the selectors may decide to take a chance on untested arbitrator Y.

Part-time or Full-time? For 80 percent of the people in the field, arbitration is a part-time occupation. It takes some time to build a practice that provides a decent living, particularly if one plans to live exclusively on earnings from arbitration. Almost all arbitrators have some other source of income. Many, of course, are full-time members of the professoriate, and most of these will remain so throughout the bulk of their working lives. Some arbitrate on a part-time basis until they retire from their primary occupation. Others undoubtedly hold on to a law or consulting practice, do training programs, or teach on an adjunct basis, some by choice and some in the hope that their practice will build.

The Arbitration Career: The Later Phases. The second part of the arbitration career was postulated to begin when that first case is decided (usually between age 42 and 48) and that it extends until the time when the career is established. For many arbitrators, entry into the NAA signifies the end of this part of the arbitration career. Entry into the NAA is considered to be the point of passage into the third phase of the career, or the journeyman years.

These are the years when arbitrators carry their peak caseloads. NAA members generally handle between fifty and seventy cases a year during this period and nonmembers, between twelve and sixteen. For most arbitrators, these years extend beyond normal retirement age. Although non-NAA arbitrators handle far fewer cases than Academy members, both groups seem to continue to operate at or near their peak caseload until well past their 60th year. Although a decline in caseload sets in at around age 70, many NAA arbitrators carry heavy caseloads even past the age of 75.

When do arbitrators leave the active practice? The answer appears to be that as long as they feel that they are physically able to do the work, they will arbitrate as long as they are selected for cases. Arbitrators seem to live to a ripe old age and arbitrate all the way to the grave. Of the 620

United States respondents to this study, only 19 (or less than 3%) had retired, and they usually retire at quite advanced ages. Arbitration is interesting work that many find personally fulfilling. Furthermore, the field is attractive to older people because arbitrators can control their schedule: they can limit their availability or allow for illness or a long vacation by removing themselves from certain lists and reinstating their names when they are ready.

Caseloads

Prior to the completion of this study, there was very little general information available on the number of cases decided by arbitrators in the United States, the kinds of cases, and where they came from. This study has filled this gap. The entire population of arbitrators decided close to 80,000 cases in 1986, with roughly 80 percent of these involving the grievances of unionized employees. The remaining 20 percent of the case-load consisted of interest cases, the grievances of non-unionized employees, fact-finding, mediation, med-arb, and forms of alternative dispute resolution work.

In 1986, four out of five active arbitrators practiced arbitration on a part-time basis. The typical full-time arbitrator averaged 65 grievances and part-timers, 14. But the distribution of cases was highly skewed: half of the cases were decided by 11 percent of the active arbitrators; the least busy 25 percent of the active arbitrators decided only 2 percent of the cases; and one arbitrator in five decided no cases at all.

Cases come to arbitrators from many sources and, contrary to the expectations of many people, the American Arbitration Association and the Federal Mediation and Conciliation Service were not the source of a majority of cases decided in 1986. These two agencies processed about 40 percent of the cases. The largest single source of arbitration cases was permanent panels and almost as many cases come to arbitrators by direct appointments as come through either the AAA or the FMCS. The number of interest cases is much smaller than the number of grievance cases, but two-thirds of the interest cases come from state panels.

The different kinds of cases seem to hang together—the arbitrator with a heavy grievance caseload tends to have a heavier load of interest cases, non-union grievances, panel memberships, direct selections, and so forth. For the most part, an arbitrator's caseload either develops quickly or develops hardly at all. Caseloads appear to be firmly established by the time arbitrators have been in the field for about five years and do not change dramatically in subsequent years. More than two out of three who enter the field never "make it big"—some by design and others by unfortunate circumstance. Although they may work at arbitration over many years, they work at it part-time and never build a large caseload—averaging at the peak of their career about eight cases a year.

Although the study design does not permit a firm conclusion to be drawn about the impact of NAA membership, the data suggest, unexpectedly, that membership alone had little effect on the caseloads of part-time arbitrators and a comparatively small effect (in the order to 10 to 20%) on the caseloads of full-time practitioners. By and large, it appears that arbitrators with heavy caseloads would have had them whether or not they were Academy members.

Earnings

Information about earnings from arbitration practices in the United States has not been widely available. The NAA study showed that there was a certain homogeneity about arbitration charges in 1986. There was relatively little difference in the per diem rates charged by full and part-time practitioners and by NAA members and nonmembers. Most arbitrators charged more for interest cases than for grievances, but not much more. Almost all arbitrators charged for hearing, study, and writing days, travel expenses, and for untimely cancellations, but few had a docketing fee or other administrative charges.

This study showed that arbitrators probably earn less money than most people think. In 1986, the typical arbitrator earned approximately $25,000 from grievance and interest arbitration, with the bulk of the earnings coming from grievances. But the study also showed that arbitration earnings differ substantially. As would be expected, NAA members earned much more than nonmembers (an average of $65,000 as opposed to $15,000), and full-time arbitrators earned much more than part-time ones (an average of $67,000 versus $15,000). But the earnings data also hinted at other, more subtle differences.

For example, the data on study time suggest that NAA arbitrators may hear more complex cases. In 1986, the typical non-NAA arbitrator spent thirteen days hearing cases and an additional seventeen in study and drafting (roughly a 1-to-1 ratio of hearing to study). On the other hand, the typical NAA arbitrator spent 45 days hearing cases and 70 in study and writing (a ratio of 1 hearing day to 1.6 study days).

Some surprising information was developed on the comparative earnings of men and women in the field. Although the average number of cases heard by women was higher, the male arbitrators earned more from each case heard. Some of the gender difference in earnings per case came from the higher per diem charged by men ($386 versus $361). But most of the difference came from the fact that the men took longer with their cases (3.0 days as opposed to 2.5). Women arbitrators tend to be much younger and less experienced than men. For this reason perhaps, they get fewer of the more complex cases requiring lengthy analysis. However, in the final analysis, the gender differences in cases heard and in earnings per case were offsetting. Thus, 1986 annual earnings from labor arbitration for men and women were about equal.

Finally, echoing the findings from the caseload chapter, arbitration earnings are markedly skewed. Almost half of the active arbitrators in the United States earned $10,000 or less from arbitration in 1986, and two-thirds earned $20,000 or less. Only 5 percent of the active arbitrators earned $100,000 or more from their practices. From an earnings viewpoint, arbitration is a risky profession.

Surplus or Shortage

The last of the substantive chapters dealt with whether there is a shortage of arbitrators in the United States. The chapter examined the surplus/shortage question from two perspectives. The first approach was based upon data provided by the arbitrators on the number of cases they wanted to hear, whether they wanted their practices to expand, and whether they had the time available to hear additional cases. The second approach combined objective data about the ratio of arbitrators to union members in various regions of the country with the arbitrators' expressions of caseload preferences. Both approaches supported the surplus rather than the shortage theory. Three major findings emerged from the analysis.

First, there is no evidence of an arbitrator shortage for the United States as a whole. The arbitrators who were active in 1986 were willing to handle a much larger caseload and had the time to do so. Availability was not restricted to the newer arbitrators or those with very small practices. About half of the NAA members wanted more cases; almost 60 percent of the full-time arbitrators wanted more cases; and more than three arbitrators in four reported that their services were underutilized. The typical arbitrator expressed a desire to hear about a dozen new cases and had space on the calendar for about fourteen. The 1986 arbitration population was willing and able to hear about 30,000 more cases—almost 40 percent more than they actually heard.

Second, there is no evidence of a shortage in any part of the country. The country was subdivided into the nine geographic regions used by the United States Bureau of the Census. In none of these geographic regions did the arbitration population report more cases than could be handled. The degree of surplus ranged from 7.1 cases per arbitrator in the West North Central states to 25.9 cases in the East South Central region.

Third, the supply and demand for arbitrators is a fluctuating one. New people continually enter the field, and the practices of the "old hands" undergo considerable change. Fifteen percent of the arbitrators who were active in 1986 had less than five years of arbitration experience. One quarter of the arbitrators reported that their practices had grown over the past five years, while 20 percent indicated a decline.

Is there a shortage of arbitrators? The data in Chapter 7 show convincingly that there is no shortage of arbitrators in the United States or, more precisely, that there was no shortage in 1986. When these data are combined with the demographic and career information in Chapters 2 and 4, it is logical to conclude that there was no shortage of arbitrators qualified to handle most labor-management disputes. The long lines and scheduling delays that so many parties complain of undoubtedly result from their desire to select from a highly restricted list. A large number of selectors are apparently more willing to wait months for a date with a mainline arbitrator than to move more quickly to a hearing with a lesser-known figure. If there is a shortage, it is a shortage of acceptable arbitrators rather than a shortage of qualified arbitrators.

Conclusions

Arbitrators: Barely Qualified or Distinguished?

Arbitration has come to play a verifiably significant role in union-management relations since the passage of the Labor Management Relations Act in 1947. Almost every private and public sector bargaining agreement contains a clause that calls for binding arbitration of grievances and a substantial number of the states have provided for interest arbitration for some of the public employee work force. Section 203(d) of the LMRA provides that "Final adjustment by a method agreed upon by the parties is hereby declared to be the desirable method for settlement of grievance disputes arising over the application or interpretation of an existing collective bargaining agreement."

In subsequent cases, from *Lincoln Mills* in 1957[2] through *Misco* thirty years later,[3] the U.S. Supreme Court has repeatedly reinforced labor arbitration as a cornerstone of the national labor policy. Most observers agree that the Court has:

(P)roperly supported the development and expansion of grievance arbitration as an efficient, fair, and inexpensive system of private industrial jurisprudence. The overwhelming majority of labor agreements provide for binding arbitration of grievance disputes and management as well as labor have come to realize that arbitration is preferable to either costly work stoppages or lengthy judicial proceedings for the resolution of grievances.[4]

At least one of the reasons for these developments has been rooted in the Court's favorable view of the labor arbitrator. A good part of the foundation for contemporary labor arbitration in the United States came from the fact that the Court saw the arbitrator as a person who, by virtue of education and experience, could be expected not only to interpret the words of a labor-management agreement in a highly specific set of factual circumstances, but also to consider the broader lives of the worker, the shop, and the organization. As Mr. Justice Douglas said in the *Steelworkers' Trilogy*:

The labor arbitrator is usually chosen because of the parties' confidence in his knowledge of the common law of the shop and their trust in his personal judgment to bring to bear considerations which are not expressed in the contract as criteria for judgment. The parties expect that his judgment of a particular grievance will reflect not only what the contract says but, insofar as the collective bargaining agreement permits, such factors as the effect upon productivity of a particular result, its consequence to the morale of the shop, his judgment whether tensions will be heightened or diminished. For the parties' objective in using the arbitration process is primarily to further their common goal of uninterrupted production under the agreement, to make the agreement serve their specialized needs.[5]

Not surprisingly, the attacks on the arbitration profession began shortly after this decision was rendered. One of the earlier, more thoughtful critiques came in the Storrs Lectures given by arbitrator Paul Hays at the Yale Law school in 1966. He noted that Justice Douglas cited "no authority whatsoever . . ." for his statements and that he knew "of no authority that would lend them support."[6] He went on to say that:

There is a surprising lack of factual studies of the arbitration process. Yet if we are to understand what the system really is and how it actually works in practice, such studies are vital. The literature of arbitration today, and it is among the dullest and dreariest, consists almost entirely of subjective discussions written by arbitrators, who are likely to know very little about arbitration outside their own practice—and about their own experience are not inclined to frankness.[7]

He then reported the results of his own brief study (from the capsule biographies of arbitrators published by *Labor Arbitration Reports*) concluding that there were only a dozen or so persons whose records revealed "any substantial distinction . . ." and that there were "astonishingly few whose past experience, other than legal training, . . ." included "anything of importance that is relevant to arbitration."[8]

This book approximates the study that Professor Hays requested so many years ago. Critically, its overall conclusion supports the Douglas view of the labor arbitrator rather than the Hays perspective. When the parties come to the hearing, the arbitrator who sits at the head of the table is typically a highly educated, well-seasoned professional. More than likely that arbitrator will be an attorney with advocacy experience in labor relations or a professor with a Ph.D. in the IR/HR field. That arbitrator will have spent several years in some facet of union-management relations other than arbitration and will bring roughly twenty years of arbitration experience to the table.

Arbitrators who practice full-time, on average, will have the experience gained from deciding almost 900 cases; if part-time, over 200 cases. Arbitrators who belong to the NAA will, on average, bring the knowledge gained in deciding almost 1,100 cases. In short, a very large number of the people who practice the profession of arbitration today possess the education, the fund of experience, and the case background envisioned in the words of Justice Douglas. Almost all of those who were active arbitrators in 1986 possessed the relevant qualifications, and a very large number offered substantial distinction. The 280 busiest arbitrators in the United States in 1986 (about 10 percent of the active population) decided an average of 107 cases that year and 1,377 over their careers.

The Labor Market Works!

The study also indicates that the market for arbitration works. There are four kinds of arbitrators in the United States:

(1) Busy full-timers with long lists of clients willing to wait for them, whose practices provide them with a fine income;

(2) Busy part-timers, combining arbitration with the demands of another position, usually professorial in nature;

(3) Newer arbitrators, whether full or part-time, whose practices are becoming established; and

(4) A large number, perhaps seventy percent, of those in the arbitration profession with very small practices.

What has happened is that the parties have made choices: they have determined what they want from an arbitrator, and the careers of the different kinds of arbitrators reflect their individual abilities to pass the parties' test of acceptability. The successful arbitrator is the one whom the losing party picks a second or a third time. Although the study did not provide information on the reasoning used in selecting arbitrators, arbitrators who make it into one of the top two classes are probably those who produce clearly written, closely reasoned decisions that, in the words of Justice Douglas:

(R)eflect not only what the contract says but, insofar as the collective bargaining agreement permits, such factors as the effect upon productivity of a particular result, its consequence to the morale of the shop, his judgment whether tensions will be heightened or diminished.

Those who fail to pass this test for whatever reason never achieve broad acceptability and their practice peaks at a much lower level. Thus, the skewed earnings and caseload distributions, disappointing as they must be to those at the left end of the scale, probably reflect a free and healthy labor market at work.

Success Factors

But the message that the NAA data send to the new arbitrator is clear. To use a show business phrase, "Don't quit your day job!" Unfortunately, the data do not paint an explicit picture of the factors associated with success.

Background characteristics appear to have little to do with it. Very few of the demographic variables in this study were shown to be related to caseloads or earnings, and whatever relationships did exist were invariably weak. This finding suggests either that new, more subtle background-related variables are needed or that success in arbitration ties more strongly into factors in the current situation. There is a pressing need for more research in this area.

The data did show that the practices of the busiest arbitrators were qualitatively as well as quantitatively different from those of other arbitrators. The busier arbitrators drew many more cases from permanent panels, permanent umpireships, and direct selection. If new arbitrators are to have ringing success as mainline arbitrators, they will not find it in the AAA, FMCS, and state panels alone. Unless arbitrators make the jump into these other sources of cases, their careers will be limited.

A Declining Caseload?

For many years people have been predicting a decline in the overall arbitration caseload. One would think that this prediction would be safe. After all, the bulk of the arbitration business comes from the grievances of unionized employees, and the number of unionized employees in the United States has gone into an absolute decline. This prediction, furthermore, is supported by the declining caseloads reported by the FMCS and the AAA cited in Chapter 5.

But the data from this study do not support that prediction. As many arbitrators reported an expanding caseload as reported a declining one. At the worst, the statistics indicate a stable caseload. This finding suggests, albeit tentatively, that some of the traditional sources of cases— mainly the FMCS and the AAA—may be diminishing somewhat in importance. Those agencies still play a substantial role, and the number of cases they process still dwarf those that come from some of the newer, emerging sources. But apparently, many arbitrators have made up losses from these sources with cases from other private and public panels, supplemented by non-arbitration work and ADR activity.

ADR and All That

Much has been written about the need for labor arbitrators to move into other forms of dispute resolution. The data from this study show that these areas have not yet taken on major significance in the practice of the majority of arbitrators. The bread and butter for today's arbitrator is the grievance case involving the unionized employee, followed distantly by interest arbitration. Perhaps one-quarter or one-third of today's arbitrators engage routinely in mediation, med-arb, fact-finding, or the arbitration of non-union grievances but the number of cases is usually small. An even smaller percentage of arbitrators have moved into ADR work.

Despite the fact that caseloads overall appear to have held fairly constant, the labor movement still is in eclipse, and the number of arbitration cases processed by the two largest agencies, the AAA and the FMCS, has been in decline. The future for many arbitrators may lie, in part, in some of these nontraditional activities. It is possible that a large part of the future of arbitration is being written in Congress and in the many state legislatures that are today considering legislation which revises traditional Employment-At-Will concepts. If the traditional doctrine that employees may be discharged for good cause, bad cause, or no cause at all is reversed or diminished in power, organizations may come to look upon arbitration as a more effective way of dealing with At-Will discharges than the courts.

Women and Minorities

A few words in closing might be stated about the excruciatingly slow rate of change in the sexual and racial demographics. Women and minorities simply have not made great inroads into this traditionally white male profession. Women and minorities have not yet entered the field in large numbers and relatively few have achieved large success (measured in terms of caseload). The problem is more severe in the case of minorities. Female arbitrators were still few in number, but they averaged very respectable caseloads. Minority arbitrators, however, were extremely few in number—too few in number to warrant comment on the size of their practices.

If the gender and racial mix problem is to be tackled effectively, arbitrators, professional societies, selectors, and the female and minority aspirants themselves have to work on it. First, individual arbitrators and local chapters of the NAA or the IRRA can make it easier for women and minorities to enter the field by expanding training efforts and apprenticeships.

Second, selectors should examine the gender and racial mix in their own ranks. Perhaps the large scale entrance of women and minorities into arbitration waits for the time when women and minorities play a more dominant role in selecting arbitrators for cases.

Finally, this study has called attention to the connection between activity in professional societies and arbitral caseload. Successful arbitrators are able to identify the correct professional societies, go to the right meetings, and perhaps use this exposure as a basis for securing the cases that ultimately lead to permanent panels and umpireships. An active attempt to increase personal visibility may be the contribution that women and minorities can make to this problem.

And in Conclusion

This study suggests that, contrary to the opinions of some, the profession of labor arbitration is still healthy. Traditional caseloads have held up reasonably well and newer areas are emerging. To a very large degree this health may result from the quality of the people who choose to enter this profession. It is a risky profession, because many who choose it never build the broad acceptability that leads to the large numbers of cases required to generate significant earnings. Many, perhaps most, however, are satisfied with their part-time commitment to the field. Either way, the people who choose this profession invariably bring to it an enriched academic background and many years of experience in a related field.

The authors and editors of this book are all seasoned arbitrators whose view of the profession may be biased because they enjoy and respect it so. Nevertheless, their interpretations of the data were an honest attempt at dispassionate objectivity.

Notes

1. This event took place on May 30, 1937, when the Chicago police attacked 300 steelworkers picketing a Republic Steel plant.

2. *Textile Workers Union v. Lincoln Mills*, 353 U.S. 448 (1957).

3. *United Paperworkers International Union v. Misco, Inc.*, 108 S. Ct. 364 (1987).

4. Joan Parker, "Judicial Review of Labor Arbitration Awards: Misco and Its Impact on the Public Policy Exception," *The Labor Lawyer* 4, no. 4 (Fall 1988), p. 684.

5. *United Steelworkers v. Warrior and Gulf Navigation Co.*, 363 U.S. at 582 (1960).

6. Paul R. Hays, *Labor Arbitration: A Dissenting View* (New Haven and London: Yale University Press, 1966), p. 37.

7. Ibid., p. 38.

8. Ibid., p. 54.

Appendix I

Questionnaire

**Study of Characteristics and Practices of
Professional Labor Arbitrators in
the United States and Canada**

**Sponsored by the
National Academy of Arbitrators and the
NAA Research and Education Foundation**

Have you ever been a neutral labor arbitrator?

___Yes

___No→ This questionnaire is to be completed by <u>neutral</u>
        labor arbitrators only. Do not complete this
        questionnaire. Please write your job title on
        the line below and return the questionnaire in
        the postage paid envelope provided. Thank you.

_____

Please answer all questions unless instructed otherwise.
Circle the number which corresponds with your answer or
fill in blanks for each question.

First, we would like some information about you, your
education, and professional affiliations.

1. Do you have a law degree?

   1 = Yes
   2 = No (Go to Question 3)

2. In what year did you receive your law degree?

   19___

3. Have you received any other degree?

   1 = Yes
   2 = No (Go to Question 7)

4. What is the highest level of education (other than a law
   degree)that you have received?

   1 = High school
   2 = Vocational, technical school
   3 = 2-year associate degree
   4 = Bachelor's degree
   5 = Graduate word
   6 = Masters degree
   7 = Ph.D.

5. In what field did you receive this degree?

_____

6. In what year did you receive this degree?

   19___

7. In what year were you born?

   19___

8. Are you ...

    1 = Male
    2 = Female

9. Are you ...

    1 = Married
    2 = Divorced or separated
    3 = Widowed
    4 = Never married

10. Are you ...

    1 = White, non hispanic
    2 = White, hispanic
    3 = Black, non hispanic
    4 = Black, hispanic
    5 = Asian
    6 = Other_____
                    (specify)

11.a) Are you a dues paying member of the following
     professional organizations?

Yes	No	
1	2	American Arbitration Association
1	2	Industrial Relations Research Assoc. (Ntl. or Local)
1	2	Society of Professional in Dispute Resolution
1	2	Society of Federal Labor Relations Professionals
1	2	The labor law section of your local or regional bar association
1	2	ABA or CBA labor law section
1	2	National Academy of Arbitrators (NAA)

  b) IF YES: In what year did you become a NAA member?

     19___

  c) Please list below any other professional organizations
     you belong to.

     _____

     _____

12.a) Where is your main office located?

_____
            (city)   (state or province)

b) When was it established? _____
                                (month/day/year)

c) Do you have any additional offices?

1 = Yes
2 = No (Go to Question 13)

d) Where are they located and what year were they
   established?

_____ _____
    (city)   (state/province)   (year)

_____ _____
    (city)   (state/province)   (year)

Next we would like some information about your career.

13. What were the two main events or experiences in your
    life which caused you to choose to become a neutral
    labor arbitrator (e.g., time as an apprentice or intern
    arbitrator; participant in a labor arbitration training
    program; work for a govt. agency, FMCS, NLRR, DOL, NWLB;
    work as an advocate, etc.)?

    _____

    _____

    _____

14. What was your principal occupation before you became
    a labor arbitrator? (circle one)

1 = Administrator with a regulatory body
2 = Administrator, Personnel, or Industrial Relations
3 = Consultant
4 = Lawyer
5 = Non arbitrating neutral, mediator, or fact finder
6 = Teacher
7 = Union Representative
8 = Other _____
                        (specify)

15. Have you ever held a fulltime job with a union or other
    labor organization?

1 = Yes → For how many years?___
2 = No

16. Have you ever held a fulltime non-union job in personnel/ industrial relations?

    1 = Yes→For how many years?___
    2 = No

17. In what year did you decide your fist case as a neutral labor arbitrator?

    19___

18. In your career as a neutral labor arbitrator, approximately how many grievance and interest cases have you decided?

    _____
    (Total lifetime cases)

This section of the questionnaire concerns you work in 1986.

19. In 1986, were you working as an arbitrator on interest and/or grievance arbitration cases, excluding other neutral work (e.g., mediation, fact finding) on a ...

    1 = Full-time basis (Go to Question 24)
    2 = Part-time basis
    3 = Not working in 1986→ Why not?_____

    _____
    Thank you for the information. Since you were not working as a neutral labor arbitrator in 1986, please return this questionnaire.

Questions 20-23 are to be answered by those working on a part-time basis in 1986.

20. In 1986, what was your principal occupation other than labor arbitrator?

    0 = None, retired from previous occupation
    1 = Administrator with regulatory body
    2 = Administrator, Personnel, or Industrial Relations
    3 = Consultant
    4 = Lawyer
    5 = Non arbitrating neutral, mediator, or fact finder
    6 = Teacher
    7 = Union Representative
    8 = Other _____
                    (please specify)

21. In 1986, approximately what percent of your total gross earned income was derived from your work as a neutral labor arbitrator?

    ____%

22. In 1986, approximately how many full-time equivalent days per month did you devote to neutral labor arbitration? (Include hearing, writing, travel, executive session days)

___days per month

23. Would you like to practice on a full-time basis?

1 = Yes
2 = No

The following questions are to be answered by everyone.

24. Please indicate the panels which you were on in 1986. (Circle all that apply.)

AD HOC PANELS

00 = None
01 = AAA
02 = FMCS
03 = State or provincial _____
                                    (specify)
04 = Others _____

_____
                    (specify)

PERMANENT PANELS

00 = None
10 = Employer/Union _____
                            (specify)
11 = Postal industry
12 = Steel industry
13 = Others _____

_____
                    (specify)

25.a) Did you hold a permanent umpireship in 1986?

1 = Yes
2 = No (Go to Question 26)

b) List the employers/unions involved.

_____

_____

_____

26.a) In 1986, how many grievance cases involving a union or employee association and an employer did you decide?

___(If NONE, Go to Question 27.a)

b) How many of these cases involved a board of neutrals or a panel where you were the neutral?

____

c) How was the total in a) distributed by listing service?

___FMCS
___AAA
___State or Provincial agency
___Permanent Panel
___Permanent Umpireship
___Direct appointment by parties
___Other (specify) _____

27.a) In 1986, how many interest arbitration cases involving a union or employee association and an employer did you decide?

____ (If NONE, Go to Question 28)

b) How many of these cases involved a board of neutrals or a panel where you were the neutral?

____

c) How was the total in a) distributed by listing service?

___FMCS
___AAA
___State or Provincial agency
___Permanent Panel
___Permanent Umpireship
___Direct appointment by parties
___Other (specify) _____

28.a) In 1986, how many cases did you decide which did not involve representation through a union or employee association?

____ (If NONE, Go to Question 29)

b) In how many of these cases were you mutually selected by the parties?

____

29. How many of you 1986 cases resulted in ...

___an advisory decision?

___a final and binding decision?

(Total should match the number in 28.a)

30. In 1986, was your caseload similar to your labor arbitration practice 5 years ago?

1 = Yes
2 = No → How was it different? _____

_____

31. Approximately how many cases did you refuse in 1986 because you were too busy to offer reasonable hearing dates and the parties could not wait?

    ____

32. Approximately how many additional cases would you have been able to schedule and decide in 1986?

    ____

33.a) In 1986, how many grievance and interest arbitration cases would you like to have decided?

    ____

   b) In 1987, how many grievance and interest arbitration cases would you like to decide?

    ____

   c) In 1990, how many grievance and interest arbitration cases would you like to decide?

    ____

   d) Please explain why you would like more or less cases in the future. _____

   _____

Next we would like some information about your fees and billing in 1986.

34. For a typical grievance arbitration case what were your 1986 fees?

   $____Per diem fee
   $____Docketing fee
   $____Cancellation fee
   $____Other fees (explain)_____

35. For a typical interest arbitration case what were your 1986 fees?

   $____Per diem fee
   $____Docketing fee
   $____Cancellation fee
   $____Other fees (explain)_____

36. Excluding expenses, what was the average amount billed for a case in 1986?

   $____

37. For each of the following activities, please report how
    many days you <u>billed</u> for in 1986.

    ____Hearing days billed
    ____Cancelled or postponed days billed
    ____Study days billed
    ____Travel days billed
    ____Executive session days billed

In this section, we would like to know about the types of
issues, the industries and location of the cases you decided
as a neutral labor arbitrator in 1986.

38. Listed below are some common grievance issues. Would you
    first circle the number which represents the three issues
    you most frequently decided on in 1986. Then on the line
    provided for each of the three issues, would you write the
    approximate number of cases you had in 1986 involving that
    issue.

    ____ 1. Absenteeism   ____22. Overtime
    ____ 2. Alcohol/drug abuse   ____23. Past practice
    ____ 3. Arbitrability   ____24. Pensions
    ____ 4. Assignment of work   ____25. Wages/salary/comp.
    ____ 5. Bargaining unit work   ____26. Reduction in force
    ____ 6. Demotion   ____27. Reporting/call-in/
    ____ 7. Discharge   callback pay
    ____ 8. Discrimination   ____28. Safety
    ____ 9. Dress code   ____29. Scheduling
    ____ 10. Environmental pay   ____30. Seniority
    ____ 11. Health/Welfare   ____31. Severance pay
    ____ 12. Holidays/holiday pay   ____32. Strike or lockout
    ____ 13. Incentive rates/standards ____33. Subcontracting
    ____ 14. Job classification   ____34. Successorship
    ____ 15. Job evaluation   ____35. Tardiness
    ____ 16. Job posting/bidding   ____36. Training
    ____ 17. Jurisdiction   ____37. Transfer
    ____ 18. Layoff/bumping/recall   ____38. Union business
    ____ 19. Management rights   ____39. Vacations/vac. pay
    ____ 20. Mergers/consolidation/   ____40. Work performance
             accretion/other plants   ____41. Working conditions
    ____ 21. New/reopened contract terms____42. Other (specify):
                                             _____

39. In the past five years, have you seen any change in the
    frequency and/or type of issues you have been deciding?

    1 = Yes→ What are these changes?_____
            _____

    2 = No

40. Approximately what percent of your 1986 grievance and arbitration cases were from the ...

___% public sector?
___% private sector?

41. Listed below are some types of industry. Would you first circle the number which represents the three industries in which you decided the most grievance and interest arbitration cases in 1986. Then on the line provided for the three industries, would you write the approximate number of cases you had in 1986 involving that issue.

PRIVATE SECTOR

___ 1. Aerospace
___ 2. Agriculture
___ 3. Airlines
___ 4. Aluminum
___ 5. Automotive
___ 6. Bakery
___ 7. Beverage
___ 8. Brass and Copper
___ 9. Brewery
___10. Broadcasting
___11. Canning
___12. Cement
___13. Chemicals
___14. Clothing
___15. Coal
___16. Communications
___17. Construction
___18. Dairy
___19. Distillery
___20. Education
___21. Electrical equipment
___22. Electronic commun.
___23. Entertainment/Arts
___24. Feed/fertilizer
___25. Food
___26. Foundry
___27. Furniture
___28. Glass
___29. Grain mill
___30. Heating/ventilation
___31. Health care
___32. Hotel/restuarant
___33. Iron

___34. Leather
___35. Lumber
___36. Machinery
___37. Manufacturing misc.
___38. Maritime
___39. Meat packing
___40. Metal fabrication
___41. Mining
___42. Nuclear energy
___43. Packaging
___44. Paint/varnish
___45. Petroleum
___46. Pharmaceuticals
___47. Plastics
___48. Plumbing
___49. Printing/publishing
___50. Pulp and paper
___51. Refrig. (air cond.)
___52. Retail stores
___53. Rubber
___54. Scientific inst./controls
___55. Services
___56. Ship building/drylock
___57. Shoe
___58. Sports
___59. Steel
___60. Stone
___61. Textile
___62. Tobacco
___63. Transportation
___64. Trucking/storage
___65. Upholstering
___66. Utilities
___67. Other:_____

PUBLIC SECTOR

___80. Federal		___83. Municipal	
___81. State		___84. School district	
___82. County		___85. Other:_____	

42. Do you see any change in the types of issues you are
deciding, by industry, compared to what you decided
five years ago?

1 = Yes→ Please explain _____

2 = No   _____

43. Listed below are some geographical locations. Would you
circle the number which represents the two locations (and
surrounding area) where you decided the greatest number
of grievance and interest arbitration cases in 1986. Then
on the line provided next to each code number, write the
number of cases you decided in each of those two locations.

USA

___ 1. Akron, OH	___34. Houston, TX
___ 2. Albany, NY	___35. Indianapolis, IN
___ 3. Albuquerque, NM	___36. Jackson, MS
___ 4. Allentown, PA	___37. Jacksonville, FL
___ 5. Anchorage, AK	___38. Kalamazoo, MI
___ 6. Atlanta, GA	___39. Kansas City, MO
___ 7. Baltimore, MD	___40. Knoxville, TN
___ 8. Birmingham, AL	___41. Las Vegas, NV
___ 9. Boston, MA	___42. Lewiston, ID
___10. Buffalo, NY	___43. Little Rock, AR
___11. Cedar Rapids, IA	___44. Long Island, NY
___12. Charlotte, NC	___45. Los Angeles, CA
___13. Chattanooga, TN	___46. Louisville, KY
___14. Cheyenne, WY	___47. Memphis, TN
___15. Cleveland, OH	___48. Miami, FL
___16. Cincinnati, OH	___49. Milwaukee, WI
___17. Chicago, IL	___50. Minneapolis, MN
___18. Columbus, OH	___51. Mobile, AL
___19. Concord, NH	___52. Nashville, TN
___20. Dallas, TX	___53. New Orleans, LA
___21. Dayton, Oh	___54. New York, NY
___22. Denver, CO	___55. Newark, NJ
___23. Des Moines, IA	___56. Oklahoma City, OK
___24. Detroit, MI	___57. Omaha, NE
___25. Erie, PA	___58. Parkersburg, WV
___26. Evansville, IN	___59. Peoria, IL
___27. Fargo, ND	___60. Philadelphia, PA
___28. Grand Rapids, MI	___61. Phoenix, AZ
___29. Great Falls, MT	___62. Pittsburg, PA
___30. Green Bay, WI	___63. Portland, ME
___31. Harrisburg, PA	___64. Portland, OR
___32. Hartford, CT	___65. Providence, RI
___33. Honolulu, HI	___66. Rapid City, SD

___67. Richmond, VA

___68. Rockford, IL

___69. Sacramento, CA

___70. Saginaw, MI

___71. St. Louis, MO

___72. Salt Lake City, UT

___73. San Diego, CA

___74. San Francisco, CA

___75. Seattle, WA

___76. South Bend, IN

___77. Springfield, MO

___78. Spokane, WA

___79. Syracuse, NY

___80. Tampa, FL

___81. Toledo, OH

___82. Trenton, NJ

___83. Washington, DC

___84. Worcestor, MA

CANADA

___101. Alberta

___102. British Columbia

___103. Federal territories

___104. Manitoba

___105. New Brunswick

___106. New Foundland

___107. Nova Scotia

___108. Ontario

___109. Prince Edward Island

___110. Quebec

___111. Saskatchewan

44. What type of arbitration training do you think you could benefit from over the next five years?

_____

_____

_____

The last few questions are related to your practice as a neutral that does not involve labor arbitration.

45.a) In 1986, were you involved in any labor-management mediation, med./arb. or fact-finding cases?

   1 = Yes
   2 = No (Go to Question 47)

  b) In 1986, how many cases did you mediate?

   ____

  c) In 1986, how many of your cases involved med./arb.?

   ____

  d) In 1986, how many of your cases involved fact-finding?

   ____

46.a) In how many alternate dispute resolution (ADR) cases were you involved as a neutral in 1986?

   ____

b) Of these 1986 ADR cases, how many were in each of the
   following sectors?

   ____Commercial
   ____Community/neighborhood
   ____Intercorporate
   ____Environmental
   ____Family/Divorce
   ____Court/annexed

   ____Other (specify) _____

c) In how many of these cases were you paid?

____

47. In the future, do you expect a greater share of your cases
    as a neutral to come from outside the area of labor
    arbitration?

    1 = Yes
    2 = No

The National Academy of Arbitrators appreciates your help with
this project. Please return this questionnaire in the postage
paid envelope provided. If you have any comments feel free to
include them below.

Appendix II

Administrative Agencies
Contacted
for
List of Arbitrators

American Arbitration Association
140 West 5th Street
New York, New York 10020

Alaska Labor Relations Agency
P.O. Box 6701
Anchorage, Alaska 99502

State of Alaska
Department of Administration
Division of Labor
Juneau, Alaska 99811

Arkansas Department of Labor
1022 High Street
Little Rock, Arkansas 72202

California Public Employment Relations Board
1031 18th Street
Sacramento, California 95814

California State Mediation and Conciliation Service
525 Golden Gate Avenue, Room 107
P.O. Box 603
San Francisco, California 94101

Colorado Division of Labor
1313 Sherman Street
#315
Denver, Colorado 80203

Connecticut State Board of Mediation and Arbitration
200 Folly Brook Boulevard
Wethersfield, Connecticut 06109

Delaware Department of Labor
Carvel Office Building
820 N. French Street
Wilmington, Delaware 19801

District of Columbia Public Employee Relations Board
415 Twelfth Street, N.W.
Suite 309
Washington, D.C. 20004

Federal Labor Relations Authority
500 C Street, S.W.
Washington, D.C. 20424

Federal Mediation and Conciliation Service
2100 K Street, N.W.
Washington, D.C. 20427

Florida Public Employees Relations Commission
2586 Seagate Drive
Turner Building, Suite 100
Tallahassee, Florida 32301

Georgia Department of Labor
501 Pulliam Street S.W., Room 525
Atlanta, Georgia 30312

Hawaii Public Employment Relations Board
550 Halekauwila Street
2nd Floor
Honolulu, Hawaii 96813

Idaho Department of Labor & Industrial Services
317 Main Street, Room 400
Statehouse Mail
Boise, Idaho 83720

Illinois Department of Labor
Conciliation & Mediation Division
100 N. First Street, Alzina Bldg., 5th Floor North
Springfield, Illinois 62706

Illinois Education Labor Relations Board
325 West Adams - 4th Floor
Springfield, Illinois 62706

Indiana Department of Labor
1013 State Office Building
100 North Senate Avenue
Indianapolis, Indiana 46204–2287

Iowa Public Employment Relations Board
507 Tenth Street
Des Moines, Iowa 50309

Kansas Department of Human Resources
512 West Sixth Street
Topeka, Kansas 66603–3178

Division of Employment Standards and Mediation
Kentucky Department of Labor
127 Building
Frankfort, Kentucky 40601

Los Angeles City Employee Relations Board
200 North Main Street
Room 1490 - City Hall East
Los Angeles, California 90012

Los Angeles County Employee Relations Commission
500 West Temple Street
Los Angeles, California 90012

Maine Labor Relations Board
State Office Building #90
Augusta, Maine 04333

Massachusetts Board of Conciliation and Arbitration
Leverett Saltonstall Building, Government Center
100 Cambridge Street, Room 1105
Boston, Massachusetts 02202

Massachusetts Labor Relations Commission
1604 Leverett Saltonstall Building
100 Cambridge Street
Boston, Massachusetts 02202

Michigan Department of Civil Service
Lewis Cass Building
320 South Walnut, Box 30002
Lansing, Michigan 28909

Bureau of Employment Relations
State of Michigan Plaza Building
14th Floor, 1200 Sixth Avenue
Detroit, Michigan 48226

Minnesota Bureau of Mediation Services
205 Aurora Avenue
Saint Paul, Minnesota 55103

Minnesota Public Employment Relations Board
Suite 205, Summit Bank Building
205 Aurora Avenue
Saint Paul, Minnesota 55101

Missouri State Board of Mediation
207 Adams Street
Jefferson City, Missouri 65101

Montana Board of Personnel Appeals
35 S. Last Chance Gulch
Helena, Montana 59620

Nassau County Public Employment Relations Board
1550 Franklin Street
Mineola, New York 11501

Nebraska Commission of Industrial Relations
301 Centennial Mall South
P.O. Box 94864
Lincoln, Nebraska 68509–4864

Public Employee Labor Relations Board
Pin Inn Plaza, Bldg. 2
117 Manchester Street
Concord, New Hampshire 03301

New Hampshire State Board of Conciliation and Arbitration
25 Maplewood Avenue
P.O. Box 360
Portsmouth, New Hampshire 03801

New Jersey Department of Labor
P.O. Box CN110
Trenton, New Jersey 08625

New Jersey Public Employment Relations Commission
495 West State Street
Trenton, New Jersey 08618

New Jersey State Board of Mediation
1180 Raymond Boulevard, Room 830
Newark, New Jersey 07102

Office of Collective Bargaining
100 Church Street
New York, New York 10007

New York State Labor Relations Board
2 World Trade Center
33rd Floor
New York, New York 10047

New York State Public Employment Relations Board
50 Wolf Road
Albany, New York 12205

North Carolina Arbitration/Conciliation Division
Department of Labor
214 West Jones Street
Raleigh, North Carolina 27603

North Dakota Department of Labor
State Capitol
Bismarck, North Dakota 58505

Oregon Employment Relations Board
Conciliation Service Division
528 Cottage Street, N.E. Suite 400
Salem, Oregon 97310

Pennsylvania Bureau of Mediation
1610 Labor & Industry Building
Harrisburg, Pennsylvania 17120

Pennsylvania Labor Relations Board
1617 Labor and Industry Building
Seventh and Forster Streets
Harrisburg, Pennsylvania 17120

Port Authority Employment Relations Panel
P.O. Box 968
Madison Square Station
New York, New York 10159

Puerto Rico Department of Labor and Human Resources
Bureau of Conciliation and Arbitration
Prudencio Rivera Martinez Building
505 Munoz Rivera Avenue
Hato Rey, Puerto Rico 00918

Puerto Rico Labor Relations Board
Box 4048
San Juan, Puerto Rico 00905

South Carolina Department of Labor
3600 Forest Drive
P.O. Box 11329
Columbia, SC 29211

Suffolk County Public Employment Relations Board
455 Wheeler Road
Route 111
Hauppauge, New York 11788

Vermont State Labor Relations Board
13 Baldwin Street
Montpelier, Vermont 05602

Virgin Islands Department of Labor
P.O. Box 890
Christiansted, St. Croix
U.S. Virgin Islands 00820

Virgin Islands Public Employees Relations Board
P.O. Box 890
Christiansted, St. Croix
U.S. Virgin Islands 00820

Washington Education Personnel Board
1202 Black Lake Boulevard, FT-11
Olympia, Washington 98504

Washington Public Employment Relations Commission
603 Evergreen Plaza Building, Mail Stop FJ-61
Olympia, Washington 98504

Waterfront Commission Employment Relations Panel
c/o P.E.R.B.
50 Wolf Road
Albany, New York 12205

West Virginia Department of Labor
1900 Washington Street, East
Charleston, West Virginia 25305

Wisconsin Employment Relations Commission
14 West Mifflin Street, Suite 200
P.O. Box 7870
Madison, Wisconsin 53707-7870

Index

About the Contributors

MARIO F. BOGNANNO is Professor and Director of the Industrial Relations Center at the University of Minnesota.

CHARLES J. COLEMAN is Professor of Management at Rutgers University.

WILLIAM H. HOLLEY, JR., is the Edward L. Lowder Professor in the College of Business at Auburn University.

JOSEPH KRISLOV is Professor of Economics at the University of Kentucky.

CLIFFORD E. SMITH is Professor Emeritus at the College of Engineering, Iowa State University.

PERRY A. ZIRKEL is a Professor in the College of Education at Lehigh University.